IN THE MEDIA
Black Portrayals
MATTER

The black female and black male in society

I0447286

RALPH CUFFEEA ALLSOPP

outskirts
press

Dedications

This book pays homage to the fully grown, fully blown, fire-breathing black women who have supported me on my journey: my grandmother, May Wilford; my mother, Lillian Cuffeea Allsopp; Aunt "Nita" Gallon; my daughters, Whitney Jackson and Renee Allsopp; my goddaughter, Elizabeth Archibald; and my colleagues and friends, Eloise Archibald, Jacqueline Bursch, Rose Dawson, Jo Anne Boyd, Palma Boyd, April Crowe, Joan Seale, Joan Cottman, Sherryl Browne Graves, Sharon Hobbs, Janice Bennet, Elizabeth Carol Webster, Secret Martin Walker, Mabel Nowell, Starla Nelson, Rosa Murray, Iris E. Scott, Pereppa Stevens, Ruth Moon, Betty Reynolds, Betty Laster, Claudie Nash, and the historical Women Warriors of Dahomey.

Legacy: Ralph Latae Allsopp, Ralph Latae Allsopp II, Timothy Chandler Allsopp, Gabriel Benjamin Allsopp, Graceson Elliot Allsopp, Nasya Davis, Whitney Allsopp Jackson, and Isabel Mays Jackson.

Mentors: Dr. Adelbert Jenkins, Sherryl Browne Graves, Dr. Eleanor Hooks, and Dr. Irving Sarnoff.

The title of this book is dedicated to Alicia Garza, Patrisse Cullors, and Opal Tometi, because it is only when black lives matter that black quarterbacks in professional football matter and black portrayals in the media matter. Thank you.

In memory of Betty Jenkins, Adrieanne Marie Griffin, PhD, my godfather Eddie Crawford, and my brothers Butch Joseph Allsopp and Carl Edward Allsopp.

TABLE OF CONTENTS

Chapter 1

INTRODUCTION AND PURPOSE OF THE STUDY

Since the advent of commercial television in the 1940s, blacks have been presented in a variety of stereotypical characterizations. This study will categorize these characterizations and examine their psychological origins and implications.

Many studies have been conducted to determine the frequency and type of portrayals afforded to black performers on network television. Dominick & Greenberg's (1970) study assessed the trend in frequency and types of portrayals for the 1967–1970 seasons. The researchers examined dramas, variety and game shows, and commercials and found a significant increase in the use of blacks in commercials over the three-year period, while black portrayals in prime-time dramas significantly increased only from 1967 to 1968. The authors also found that the proportion of blacks playing major roles rose from 8 percent to 47 percent in daytime television, while blacks in major roles declined from 63 percent to 20 percent in prime-time television over the three years. The authors concluded that, by 1970, the trend of casting more blacks for television had leveled off, except for secondary or supporting roles in prime-time dramas, and that roles played by blacks were military and law enforcement characterizations that white actors could portray.

Churchill Roberts (1970) also conducted a study to determine whether television's portrayals of blacks were depicting an honest view of black life in America. Like Dominick & Greenberg (1970), Roberts wanted to test one of the notions Martin Maloney (1968) had articulated regarding television's portrayals of blacks: (1) TV could revert to presenting *Amos 'n Andy* stereotypes, (2) TV could develop new and original stories about blacks dealing with unique problems, or (3) blacks could be placed in what had formerly been roles for white actors.[1]

By observing programs and evaluating the occupational roles black actors portrayed, Roberts (1970) sought to determine whether TV was distorting the black man's true image. His findings indicated that blacks were most often seen in occupations related to law enforcement, overrepresented in the professional category, and underrpresented in menial or blue-collar jobs, based on national figures from the US Census Bureau.

Roberts (1970) had difficulty assessing his data, because he was aware that the medium of television had also distorted occupational frequencies of whites in the same direction as blacks. He concluded that TV was not giving a true picture of blacks

---

1 M. Maloney, "Black Is the Color of Our New TV," *TV Guide*, November 16, 1968, 7.

but a more positive, socially integrative one than what they were experiencing in the real world. Roberts (1970) apparently sought to answer a much more important question related to the effect of television's portrayals on its viewing audience.

Franklin Fearing (1947) suggested that, through film, a person comes to understand who he is, his social role, and his group's values. Roberts' (1970) data suggests these same notions, but it was left up to other investigators to further verify Fearing's (1947) ideas, particularly as they related to American blacks.

In 1972, the Congressional Black Caucus issued the following statements: (1) the social and occupational progress of blacks was being hindered by the negative stereotypes on TV; (2) negative stereotypes teach blacks self-hate, consequently destructive self-images; and (3) negative stereotypes create and reinforce the myth of white superiority.[2]

Greenberg & Hanneman (1970) found that antagonistic whites (1) perceived more blacks on TV, (2) believed TV to be fairer to blacks, and (3) more regularly viewed programs that did not feature blacks than more liberal white viewers did. The writers also found that blacks (1) watched more programs featuring blacks, (2) thought TV was less fair to blacks and Latin Americans in newscasts, and (3) thought television gave more realistic portrayals of blacks than whites did. This study is not cited to disparage Hinton's (1973) study, but to suggest that the contradictory views of Hinton (1973) and his colleagues, versus the Black Caucus, may indeed be due to social and racial orientation. Both groups,

---

2 Congressional Black Caucus, "A Position on the Mass Communications Media," Washington, DC, mimeographed, 1972.

however, would agree that blacks must be portrayed positively, not only to their benefit but to that of whites as well.

Greenberg (1973) found that both black and white children tended to identify with TV blacks. Television's exposure of blacks to whites contributed to this identification, whereas personal exposure did not. Greenberg also found that TV influenced children's beliefs that TV blacks were true-to-life, while personal contact with blacks did not. Greenberg's (1973) study also pointed to the impact of television on children in their attitudes and subsequent interactions with people of different ethnic groups. By showing white and black children cartoons that were regularly broadcast on the major networks, Graves (1975) demonstrated that racial attitudes of black and white children could be influenced either positively or negatively depending on (1) the focus of the visual presentation, (2) the gender of the characters and the viewers, and (3) the number of racial characters (types) present in the presentation.

If television does assert a powerful influence over the attitudes and values of its viewers, particularly children, we must further clarify the issue of negative stereotyping. Clark (1972) suggested that minority groups go through three phases when being presented on TV: (1) nonrecognition, being scarcely seen at all; (2) ridicule, in the context of comedies that seek to satirize family and social interactions of the ethnic group; and (3) regulation, having members of the ethnic group portray characters such as policemen sworn to uphold the law and attesting to racial equality in the society.

In a related study, Jefferson (1970) isolated several aspects of black programs he considered detrimental to the image of black people:

(1) hyper-sexual characters, (2) independent female characters with no male counterparts, (3) black males presented as children, (4) asexual characters, (5) highly aggressive characters, and (6) characters who were not involved in their environment's racist aspects.

Now we must systematically evaluate programs with black performers over an extended period of time, using the categories Clark (1972) and Jefferson (1970) suggested, to determine whether these negative stereotypes occur significantly. Testing these notions is important, because filmed media, like projective tests, are not just fixed patterns of stimuli to which individuals passively respond. Their responses are active ones, determined by the individual's background and needs. In addition, visual media very effectively helps individuals understand themselves, their social roles, and their group values (Fearing, 1947).

To the extent that blacks appear in filmed media, we must evaluate the content of the material shown, as opposed to what they must see about themselves and what whites need to see about blacks. Historically, blacks have been treated not as people but as (1) property, (2) beasts of burden, (3) breeding animals, (4) diabolical, (5) unintelligent, (6) insensitive to pain, (7) superathletes, and (8) hypersexed entities with no strong family ties.

These treatments have made it hard for black people to adopt the American system of values and still see themselves as viable human beings. They do not need TV to present the above notions about blacks as fodder for public consumption, nor do they need stereotyped portrayals that decimate their self-image. Simultaneously, most whites must be reeducated about the importance of blacks in America and must not be deceived by programs derogatory to African Americans. This study will psychologically examine the incidence of blacks in prime-time programming over a thirteen-year period (1963 to 1976) and will analyze these programs according to three categories: (1) obliteration, (2) defamation, and (3) disembodiment.

Virgil Vogel (1968) first used these categories in his quest to characterize the maltreatment of Native Americans in public school textbooks. After examining more than one hundred textbooks, he determined that historians used four principal methods to either create or perpetuate inaccurate impressions of the Native American: (1) obliteration, (2) defamation, (3) disembodiment, and (4) disparagement. He believed the use of these methods was not deliberate but rather the result of prejudicial thinking and culturally determined assumptions. To him, obliteration was the complete elimination of Native American presence from historical events; defamation occurred when Native Americans were defined as subhuman savages without a balanced description of their human qualities, family life, or culture, and when describing them as intellectually inferior; and disparagement referred to the historians' denial of the extensive contributions Native Americans made to American culture.

As stated above, for this study a more extensive rating system was devised using Vogel's (1968) findings, made applicable to blacks and the treatment accorded them on prime-time television.

Chapter 2
HYPOTHESES
TO BE TESTED

H1: Between the 1963 and 1976 television seasons of the major networks, significantly more black actors will be in white roles than in black roles (characterizations) during prime-time viewing hours.

H2: Between the 1963 and 1976 seasons of the major networks, significantly more black actors will be in regulatory roles than in nonregulatory roles during prime-time viewing hours.

H3: Between the 1963 and 1976 seasons of the major networks, significantly more programs with black actors will last one season or less than programs without black actors lasting one season or less.

H4: Between the 1963 and 1976 seasons of the major networks, a significant absence of black leading characters will be on those programs employing black actors during prime-time viewing hours.

H5: Between the 1963 and 1976 seasons of the major networks, black characters will employ a significant incidence of devious behavior in their interactions with each other during prime-time viewing hours.

H6: Between the 1963 and 1976 seasons of the major networks, a significant incidence of black actors will be in supporting and/or minor roles during prime-time viewing hours.

H7: Between the 1963 and 1976 seasons of the major networks, a significant incidence of black characters will engage in sociopathic activities during prime-time viewing hours.

H8: Between the 1963 and 1976 seasons of the major networks, a significant number of black characters will interact with their families in satirical ways for the sake of humor during prime-time viewing hours.

H9: Between the 1963 and 1976 seasons of the major networks, a significant number of black families will be presented as matriarchal and/or dominated by the mother during prime-time viewing hours.

H10: Between the 1963 and 1976 seasons of the major networks, there will be a significant absence of ongoing male-female relationships featuring black characters during prime-time viewing hours.

H11: Between the 1963 and 1976 seasons of the major networks, a significant incidence of black characters will be portrayed as asexual or hyposexual during prime-time viewing hours.

H12: Between the 1963 and 1976 seasons of the major networks, a significant number of black female characters will be portrayed as unattractive 'mammy' types during prime-time viewing hours.

H13: Between the 1963 and 1976 seasons of the major networks, a significant number of black characters will be portrayed as highly intelligent during prime-time viewing hours.

H14: Between the 1963 and 1976 seasons of the major networks, there will be a significant incidence of strong, independent (black) female characters on those programs where there is an absence of an ongoing black male-black female relationship during prime-time viewing hours.

Chapter 3

METHOD

Sample

The sample comprised a list of television programs with black performers shown on the major networks from the fall of 1963 to the spring of 1976. The Avery-Knodel TV Network Guide, *TV Guide* magazine, and the television medium were the primary sources for the collected sample.

Apparatus

The apparatus consisted of a devised scoring system to rate television programs that employed black actors on the basis of their presenting or not presenting specific negative stereotypes. This scoring system was divided into three major categories:

1. **Obliteration.** The content is viewed as an amalgamation of blacks and whites. The actor is black, but his attitudes and/or the plots are foreign to the black experience. The roles could be played by a white actor. The role features the black actor as

a protector of the sociopolitical system. Programs show blacks in minor roles. Programs last one season or less.

2. **Defamation.** Programs call attention to the faults of blacks and condemn them to a status of inferiority. Shows are based on the format of *Amos 'n Andy*, a popular radio and TV show airing from 1928 to 1960 that depicted blacks as happy-go-lucky, devious, infantile, and semiliterate.[3] Programs show blacks as criminals, use black family interactions as satire, and give blacks supporting roles to white lead. Such an association lends a mysterious, intriguing quality to the white character but hardly ingratiates the black character with the viewing audience (also known as "the Huck Finn fixation").[4]

3. **Disembodiment.** The content acknowledges the existence of blacks in terms of their asexuality. Programs portray blacks as sexually incomplete and black females as unattractive. Ongoing relationships are absent. Programs have attractive, independent female characters with no corresponding male counterparts, as well as highly intelligent yet hyposexual characters.

Procedure

The following method was used to obtain the amount of time the major networks allotted to prime-time shows with black performers:

Prime-time hours are designated by the networks as the times when most people watch TV. Prime hours run from 7:30 p.m.

---

3 L. King, *Confessions of a White Racist* (New York: Viking Press, 1971), 5.
4 Donald Bogle, *Toms, Coons, Mulattoes, Mammies & Bucks* (New York, 1974), 197.

to 11:00 p.m. Monday through Saturday and from 7:00 p.m. to 11:00 p.m. Sunday. The major networks—ABC, CBS, and NBC—each have a maximum of twenty-five hours of prime-time programming per week. All three networks have a maximum total of seventy-five hours of prime-time programming per week.

Since any show could vary in duration from one-half hour to an hour to an hour and a half, it was decided to divide each network's maximum prime-time viewing into half-hour units, yielding fifty half-hour units per week instead of twenty-five hour units and a maximum total of 150 half-hour units per week instead of seventy-five hour units. For example, if a network had five hours per week of programs with black performers, those hours would be converted into ten half-hour units, and the percentage of prime time these shows occupied would be calculated based on the fifty half-hour units available to the network for the week. In this example, ten units/fifty units would be 20 percent; that is, the station had allotted 20 percent of its weekly prime-time viewing hours to programs containing at least one black performer.

To compute the percentage of prime time allotted to programs with black performers for thirteen of the last television seasons, the analysis started with the 1963–64 season and ended with the 1975–76 season. The programs, the seasons, and the amounts of time they were on the air were discovered through the Avery-Knodel TV Network Guides, *TV Guide* magazine, *Variety*, and other source materials from the Television Information Office (New York City), which is supported by the three major networks (ABC, CBS, and NBC), individual commercial stations, educational stations, and the National Association of

Broadcasters. Each program was located and correctly identified, and the percentage of prime-time hours was computed. Then each program's content was analyzed according to the scoring system designed to locate specific stereotypes that could have a negative impact on the self-concept of black viewers and foster a prejudicial position in the white viewing audience.

In addition, the types of roles given to blacks were analyzed for the 1967–68 and 1968–69 seasons, which followed the civil riots of 1967 and the subsequent clamor to have more blacks on the television screen. The types of roles in the 1970–71 and 1975–76 seasons were also analyzed because they had the two highest percentage ratings of programs with black performers. The role analysis aimed to determine whether role quality had increased along with role quantity.

Though many of the programs could be observed as either current programming or reruns, unfortunately some of the earlier shows could be evaluated from only a combination of written critiques and memory. However, no program was scored unless it had been viewed at least three times.

It should be understood that this was an exploratory study and, if replicated, should employ more than one rater with high inter-judge reliability among them. Also, at least three films of each program should be obtained for viewing and scoring purposes.

Chapter 4
RESULTS

TABLE 1

Percentages of Major Network Prime Time Allotted to Programs with Black Performers, 1963-1976

Networks

Seasons	ABC	CBS	NBC	Average Total
1963–64	0%	6%	6%	4%
1964–65	1%	0%	8%	3%
1965–66	3%	10%	8%	7%
1966–67	0%	12%	12%	8%
1967–68	4%	18%	18%	13.3%
1968–69	17%	16%	14%	15.6%
1969–70	15%	12%	15%	14%
1970–71	28%	19%	19%	22%

1971–72	16%	12%	20%	16%
1972–73	24%	16%	21%	20.3%
1973–74	21%	14%	18.5%	17.8%
1974–75	24%	10%	15.5%	16.5%
1975–76	31%	14%	20%	21.6%

Table 1

Table 1 shows the average allotment of prime-time hours occupied by programs with black performers for each network and for all major networks for the 1963–64 season through the 1975–76 season.

The table indicates a small, fluctuating number of programs with black performers in the seasons before 1966–67. The start of the 1967–68 season saw an increase in such programs to the level to which programs with black performers had not fallen below the 13.31 percent level achieved during that season. The range of major network allotment was from 3 percent at the peak viewing time in the 1964–65 season to 22 percent in the 1970–71 season.

FIGURE 1

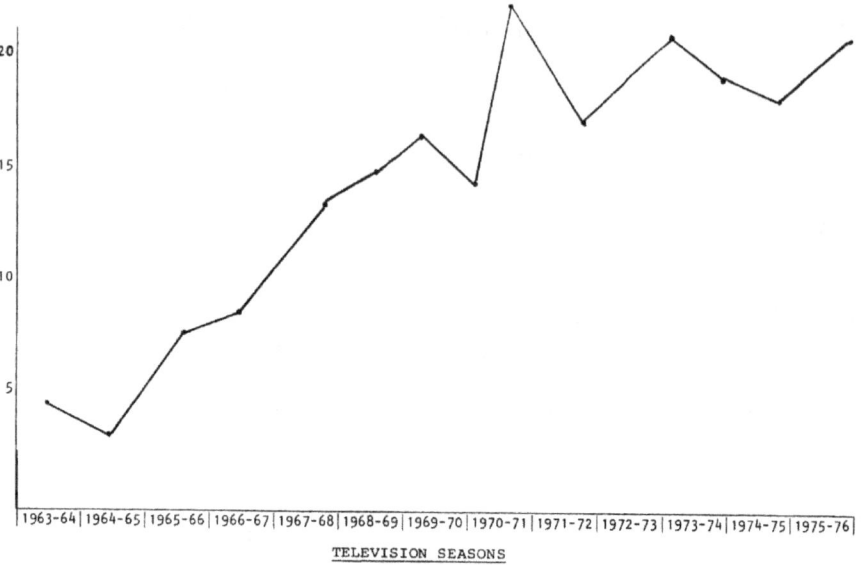

TELEVISION SEASONS

Figure 1. Percent of Major Network Prime Time Allotted to Programs with Black Performers, 1963–64 to 1975–76.

Figure 1

Figure 1, a pictorial representation of the average percentage of major network time allotted to prime-time programs in which blacks appeared, graphically illustrates the generally increasing number of programs employing black performers after the 1964–65 season. This programming trend reached its peak in the 1970–71 (22 percent), 1972–73 (20.3 percent) and 1975–76 (21.6 percent) seasons.

TABLE 2

Types of Shows on which Blacks Appeared from 1963–64 to 1975–76

Type of Program	Number of Programs	Percentage of Programs
Variety show	13	14.8
Situation		
Comedy	25	28.4
Drama	48	54.5
Professional		
Collegiate		
Sports (football, baseball, tennis, soccer)	1	2.3
Total	87	100.0

Table 2

Table 2 charts the types of shows on which blacks appeared from the 1963–64 season to the 1975–76 season.

The major type of show offering black performers employment was dramatic in nature, comprising 54.5 percent of the programs. Situation comedies (sitcoms) were the second most frequent vehicle for displaying black performers, encompassing 28.4 percent of the available programs. Variety shows were less frequent, comprising 14.8 percent of the programs. Professional sports were least frequent, comprising 2.3 percent of the prime-time programming.

In terms of numbers, blacks have either hosted or appeared as regulars on only thirteen variety shows, or an average of one show per season.

Professional sports is also a deceptive category. While such programs did not prevail over the thirteen-year period, many of the programs that did appear lasted as long as three hours (six half-hour units), and at times they were broadcast on the networks outside of the prime-time hours about four times a week.

TABLE 3

Role Analysis of the 1967–68 Television Season

2 Detectives	*N.Y.P.D., Ironside*
1 Girl Friday	*Mannix*
1 POW (radio operator)	*Hogan's Heroes*
1 Veterinarian's Assistant	*Daktari*
2 Secret Agents	*I Spy, Mission: Impossible*
1 Communications Officer (female)	*Star Trek*
African Natives	*Tarzan, Cowboy in Africa*

Role Analysis of the 1968–69 Television Season

1 Neurosurgeon 1 Housewife	*Peyton Place*
4 Detectives	*Mod Squad, N.Y.P.D.,* *Felony Squad, Ironside*
1 Nurse	*Julia*
1 Girl Friday	*Mannix*
1 Secret Agent	*Mission: Impossible*
1 Bounty Hunter	*Outcasts*
1 Communications Officer (female)	*Star Trek*
1 Rocket Copilot	*Land of the Giants*
1 POW (radio operator)	*Hogan's Heroes*

Types of Shows: 1967–68   Types of Shows: 1968–69

Drama	09	Drama	11
Sitcom	01	Sitcom	02
Variety	02	Variety	02

Table 3

Table 3 is the occupation role analysis of the 1967–67 and 1968–69 television seasons.

As the number of roles increased, they also became more varied. Roles considered regulatory in nature also increased. During these seasons, drama shows featured blacks most frequently, while few variety shows or sitcoms used black performers.

TABLE 4

Role Analysis of the 1970–71 Television Season

2 Lawyers	*Barefoot in the Park, Julia*
1 Law Student (female)	*Young Lawyers*
3 Detectives	*The Mod Squad, Ironside, McCloud*
1 District Attorney	*The Protectors*
1 Girl Friday	*Mannix*
1 Police Officer (female)	*Dan August*
1 Secret Agent	*Mission: Impossible*
1 Physical Education Teacher	*The Bill Cosby Show*
1 American History Teacher 1 Guidance Counselor (female)	*Room 222*
1 Medical Intern	*The Interns*
1 Businessman 1 College Student 1 Housewife	*The Jeffersons*
1 Nurse	*Julia*
1 Blacksmith	*Young Rebels*
2 Psychiatrist's Assistants (male, female)	*Matt Lincoln*
1 POW (radio operator)	*Hogan's Heroes*

Types of Shows:

Drama	13
Sitcom	06
Variety	03

TABLE 4A

Role Analysis of the 1976–76 Television Season

2 Delinquents	*Welcome Back, Kotter, The Cop and the Kid*
3 Police Officers	*McCloud, S.W.A.T., The Rookies*
6 Detectives	*Bronk, Police Woman, McCloud, Barney Miller, Starsky & Hutch, The Streets of San Francisco*
1 Barber	*That's My Mama*
1 Bartender	*Starsky & Hutch*
2 Pimps	*Joe Forrester, Baretta*
1 Civil Prisoner	*On the Rocks*
1 Businessman 1 Interracial Couple 1 Maid 1 College Student	*The Jeffersons*
3 Housewives	*The Jeffersons, That's My Mama, Good Times*
2 Matriarchal Characters	*That's My Mama, The Jeffersons*
1 Schoolteacher 1 Legal Secretary 1 Grandfather	*Grady*

2 Postmen	*That's My Mama, Chico and the Man*
2 Junkmen	*Sanford and Son*
1 Laborer (usually unemployed)	*Good Times*
1 Chef 1 Young War Veteran	*Beacon Hill*

Types of Shows:

Drama	09
Sitcom	10
Variety	01

Tables 4 and 4A

Tables 4 and 4A provide the occupation role analysis of the programs for the 1970–71 and 1975–76 television seasons.

In 1970–71, programs with black performers showed an increase in the variety and quality of the roles black actors were given, as well as an increase in the roles written for black female actors. Both drama and sitcoms increased in number (13 and 6, respectively), and one more variety show was added to the schedule as compared to the 1967–68 season.

In 1975–76, blacks began to appear in roles associated with white-collar professions, as well as roles that depicted them as outside the acceptable legal and social limits of society—juvenile delinquents, pimps, convicts. Regulatory and domestic roles also increased for them. That season, sitcoms (mainly about black families) outnumbered more serious dramatic presentations. Variety shows, however, remained consistently few in number.

TABLE 5

Characteristics of Roles Assigned to Black Performers on Prime-Time Programming, 1963–1976

Stereotypical Categories	Number of Programs	Percentage of Programs
Obliteration (Major category)	72	94.7**
Subcategories		
Absence of black leading characters+	72	84.7**
Black actors in white roles	48	63.0*
Black actors in regulatory roles	31	40.8
Series duration of one season or less	38	50.0
Defamation (Major category)	63	82.0**
Subcategories		
Devious behavior (Amos 'n Andy syndrome)	06	7.8
Black second banana (Huck Finn fixation), supporting/ minor roles	52	68.4*
Sociopathic behavior	07	9.2
Satirical family interactions	13	17.1

+ Including variety shows
* .02 significance
**.001 significance

Stereotypical Categories	Number of Programs	Percentage of Programs
Disembodiment (Major Category)	63	82.0**
Subcategories		
Family dominated by mother	06	7.8
Absence of ongoing male-female relationships	59	77.6*
Asexual (hyposexual)characters	52	68.4*
Unattractive (mammy-type) females	12	15.7
Highly intelligent characters	26	34.2
Independent characters (female)	11	14.6

++ Scored only in the absence of an ongoing relationship
* .02 significance
**.00l significance

Table 5

Table 5 shows the characteristics of roles assigned to black performers on major network prime-time programming during the thirteen seasons from 1963–64 to 1975–76.

Table 5 indicates the number of programs included in each of the three major categories—obliteration, defamation, disembodiment—along with the number of programs counted in each subcategory. The sum of each group of subcategories exceeds the number of programs scored for each major category, because many programs could be scored for more than one subcategory of a particular major category, but such programs were scored only once for the major category.

Table 5 also indicates the number of major and subcategories exceeding the .05 significance level. All major categories were significant, while only the subcategories of (1) absence of black leading characters, (2) black actors in white roles, (3) black second bananas, (4) absence of ongoing male-female relationships, and (5) asexual characters exceeded the .05 significance level.

TABLE 6

Results of the Chi-Square Significance Tests for Role Characteristics of Black Performers on Prime-Time Programming, 1963–1976

Categories	Percent of Programs		Significance Level	Strength of Relationship
Absence of ongoing relationships	77.6	13.08	.001+	.42
Asexual (hyposexual) characteristics	68.4	6.54	.02+	.297
Regulatory roles	40.8	1.95	.2	-
Absence of black portrayals in regulatory roles	93.5	23.5	.001+	.74
Huck Finn fixation	68.4	6.54	.02k	.297
Absence of black leading characters	84.7	40.05	.001+	.71
Absence of black portrayals (all programs)	63.0	6.08	.02+	.29

+Exceeds the .05 significance level.

Table 6

Table 6 shows the results of the Chi-Square significance test for the role characteristics of black performers on prime-time programs during the thirteen-year period of 1963–64 to 1975–76. The results show that the three major classifications of negative stereotyping—obliteration, defamation, disembodiment—were all significant at the .001 level.

Obliteration. The major contributors to this category were the subcategories of (1) absence of black leading characters (p < .001), and (2) the use of black actors in roles for white characters (p < .02). The use of black actors in regulatory roles and in series lasting one season or less was not significant in number.

Defamation. Under this category, the high incidence of blacks appearing in secondary roles was significant (p < .02), while the incidences of devious behavior between black characters, sociopathic activities, and satirical family interactions were not significant in their occurrence.

Disembodiment. Under this category, the absence of ongoing male-female relationships among black characters (p < .001) and the number of asexual characterizations (p < .02) were significant. The other subcategories—family dominated by the mother, unattractive female characters, highly intelligent characterizations, and the independent female characterizations in the absence of male counterparts—did not occur to a significant degree.

Chapter 5

DISCUSSION OF THE PSYCHOLOGICAL AND HISTORICAL FOUNDATIONS OF BLACK CHARACTERIZATIONS ON TV

Five of the stated fourteen hypotheses were found to be statistically significant, and all three major categories of which the hypotheses were components—obliteration, defamation, and disembodiment—were found to be significant. In no instance was the incidence of any subcategory zero. Of the hypotheses not found to be significant, H5, H8, H9, H12, and H14 bear further discussion:

H5: Devious behavior blacks employed in their interactions with one another;

H8: Satirical black family interactions that provoke humor;

H9: Black families presented as matriarchal and/or dominated by the female (mother);

H12: Black females presented as unattractive and/or 'mammy' types;

H14: Strong, independent black female characters on programs with no viable black male–black female relationships.

While family situation programs comprised a small number of the total programs surveyed—11.5 percent, or ten programs—seven of these had characters interacting in satirical ways that provoked humor (H8). Six family programs had characters acting in devious ways (H5), six had families dominated by the mother (H9), and six programs had an unattractive female (H12). Programs that showed a strong, independent black female (H14) were *Room 222*, *Julia*, *Mannix*, *Get Christie Love*, *Star Trek*, *Young Lawyers*, *Dan August*, and *Matt Lincoln*. Seven of these eight programs had no complementary black male (including *Julia*, which had no male counterpart until its final season).

When the hypotheses were analyzed on the basis of all surveyed programs, they were not found to be significant. However, if these hypotheses were scored for only those programs in which it was possible for them to occur, the number of significant hypotheses would have been higher. The incidence rate for programs in which it was possible for these hypotheses to occur ranged from 60 to 88 percent.

The hypotheses found to be significant were as follows:

H1: Black actors appearing in white roles;

H4: Absence of blacks in leading roles;

H6: Large incidence of supporting and minor roles.

H10: Absence of ongoing black male–black female relationships.

H11: Black characters portrayed as asexual or hyposexual.

These findings show that televised media do perpetuate negative black stereotypes. More important, however, is the question: Why have these stereotypes continued to exist? Is there a conscious effort to present blacks in derogatory ways? Or is the answer embedded in the long-standing attitudes and ideas whites have about blacks?

Two of the statistically significant hypotheses (H10 and H11) confront the question of black sexuality: the ways blacks are sexually presented on television seem intimately related to the fears and fantasies whites have about the black female, the black male, and the white female. What are these fears and fantasies? Where did they come from? To answer these questions, we must understand the relationship between blacks and whites from the point at which they first encountered one another.

When European explorers landed on the coast of Africa, many strange reports went back to Europe about the nature of the beings "discovered" there. The Europeans described the Africans as half-man, half-beast forms with human faces, long tails, and large genitals.[5] By unfortunate coincidence, English explorers had discovered the ape at about the same time. Reports came back to Europe about an animal with human characteristics and black men with beast-like traits. Stories also circulated about Africans engaging in sex with apes, possessing large genitalia, and being sexually superior to whites.[6] Whether these stories were true or not, many Europeans deemed them valid and began the myth of the sexually aggressive ape-man of Africa. In fact, many people still imagine themselves "behaving in ape-like fashion during intercourse and see themselves mounting their partners ... and carrying them away with an outpouring of grunting and primeval ecstasy."[7]

To the extent that African males had been mistakenly associated with the ape, people presumably fantasized about the apelike manner in which black males partook in sexual intercourse. Perhaps this fantasy accounts for the popularity of Edgar Rice Burroughs' Tarzan, the white ape-man and lord of the jungle. Such a character made it easier for whites to identify with his animal-like characteristics and not be in conflict with his color.

Long before blacks were discovered in Africa, the color black had already been associated with evil. Joel Kovel, in his book *White Racism: A Psychohistory*, gives historical background for his theory of black-white social-sexual interactions. In the sixteenth century, before blacks were brought to the New World, the word *black* had the following meanings: soiled, dirty, foul, deadly, horrible, wicked, atrocious, malignant, and having a dark and deadly

---

5 Jordan, *White Over Black* (North Carolina, 1968), 29.
6 Loc. cit.
7 Dally, *The Fantasy Game* (New York, 1975), 1.

purpose. In general, the color black was closely associated with the concept of badness.

When the Europeans could not explain the pigmentation of the African's skin scientifically, they resorted to the Bible to give them the answer, which was embodied in the "curse of Ham." As the Bible would have it, Ham had seen his father naked. To punish Ham, God willed that Ham's son, Chus (or Canaan), and all his descendants would be black and banished from sight. Ham's crime was more than looking at his naked father. It symbolized a blatant rejection of parental authority and acquisition of the father's sexual choice. In effect, Ham had castrated his father. Ham's brother, Noah, who did not look upon his father, gained God's approval and protection. The bad son was scarred with the black curse and banished until such time as the European explorers (descendants of the white sons of Noah) chanced upon him in Africa.[8] A son named Chus would be born to Ham, and not only he but also all of his children after him would be so black and loathsome it might remain a spectacle of disobedience to the world. And from this black and cursed Chus came all of the black Moors who are in Africa.[9]

To many Europeans, the color black and the people who were colored black symbolized the devil and the embodiment of all that was evil. Closely associated with the idea that black is evil is the idea that white, the polar opposite of black, symbolizes innocence, virginity, peace, heavenly light, and God Almighty.[10] From these beginnings, the idea that blacks were evil and linked

---

8 Jordan, 41.
9 Loc. cit.
10 Joel Kovel, *White Racism: A Psychohistory* (New York, 1970), 65.

to Satan, and whites were good and associated with God, became embedded in the minds of Europeans and Americans, and this idea has been handed down through the centuries to the present.

When blacks were brought to the New World, the notions that they were 'evil' and 'sexually excessive' traveled with them. In the South, where institutionalized slavery was a major part of the economy, white males feared the black male's sexuality but in many instances were enraptured by the sensuality of the black female. Indeed, the black female may have been more passionate than the white female, but not for any genetic reason. In the stylized culture of the pre-Civil War South, the white female was worshipped as the purest, least vital, least sexual of females. To the extent that she went along with these notions, the white female lost two important joys of womanhood: (1) the expression of passion in lovemaking, and (2) the nursing of her infants. Both of these joys were rendered to the black female.[11]

The aristocratic Southern male was split in his affection between a warm, impure black mammy, among whose people he would later seek sexual pleasure, and the pure but emotionally cold white mother, whom he would idealize. He would later defend her virtue by killing and castrating any black he imagined to be desirous of a white woman.[12] The black male became invested with desire for white women, prodigious in his sexual capacities, and the envy of all who dominated him. The white male's frustrated desire to make passionate love to the white female found its outlet via projecting these wishes onto the black male. The white female of the antebellum South also fantasized about being passionately

11 Kovel, p. 69.
12 Kovel, p. 70.

ravished by the savage ape-man (black male). Authors such as Kovel (1970) have attempted to explain the black-rape-fantasy syndrome by employing the theory of the Oedipus complex as a cultural model.

We have seen the pattern: blackness is bad; what goes on in the dark comes from the dark, thus makes the black man represent both father and son in their destructive aspects. There is evidence for this in the structure of his social role. He is the bad father who possesses the (impure) black mammy, and he has the genital power that forever excites the child's envy. He is also the bad child who lusts after the pure, utterly forbidden white mother (made sexless in reality). By making the rape fantasy the cornerstone of his culture, the white male merely repeats in adulthood the central incest taboo of his childhood. And here Southern culture makes its unique contribution to an ageless human problem: The Southern white male simultaneously resolves both sides of the conflict by keeping the black man submissive and by castrating him when submission fails. In both of these cases—in one, symbolically; in the other, directly—he is castrating the father as he once wished to do, and he also identifies with the father by castrating the son as he once feared for himself. All he must do to maintain this delectable situation is to structure his society so he directly dominates black men.[13]

Under such a model, as Kovel (1970) describes, the black man retains his sexuality but is not permitted to gain power in the social, economic or political spheres. Thus whites may subtly encourage black promiscuity and remove any power black men

---

13 Kovel, 73–74.

may have—and with it the superego structures that evolve from identifying with power—thus freeing the black male to sexually express himself. Whites may also encourage aggressiveness in blacks and structure the environment so the aggression can only gain expression with other blacks. Such behavior among blacks has not only given whites vicarious enjoyment but also kept the aggression from becoming sublimated or directed against whites.[14] Kardiner & Ovesey (1968) have labeled black-on-black aggression as an expression of self-hate without fully considering the notion that it is displaced aggression. This type of aggression can be expressed against only one's own kind for fear of the massive retaliation of discharging aggressive impulses directly at the oppressor.

The only victors are the white males, who pay the price of guilt, the specific Oedipal emotion. This guilt, unconscious in the white male, was experienced as suffering in the black female, vilification of the black male, sexually and maternally frustrating in the white female, and in the further distortion of culture's aberrant attitudes regarding black people.[15] The black-rape fantasy evolved out of the social climate of the antebellum South and was diffused throughout the country. This fantasy and its attendant fear components have been deeply embedded in the white's desire to maintain superiority and foster black submission.

Another concept that contributes to the formulation of attitudes toward blacks is "thingification" (Kovel, 1970), which is defined as reducing or dehumanizing a person to the status of a thing or object that can be treated as property. According to psychoanalytic

---

14 Kovel, 73.
15 Loc. cit.

theory, the process of dehumanization has excremental implications that can be explained by Freud's psychosexual stage of anality, as Kovel explains:

> Anal Phase ... certain nuclear ideas, such as those revolving about the concepts of *dirt* and *property*, take hold of the personality during this stage of development, and remain throughout life associatively linked to the idea of excrement. Thus, to the child, dirt corresponds to that which is hated in his excremental activities. This becomes symbolically generalized to include anything which can be associated with what comes out of the body. On the other hand, property is considered to be the loved part of his excrement, the part that he wishes to take back into himself or to give to those he loves. Excrement becomes the unconscious link in later life between these notions ... It is important in discussing racism because anality is the form of drive behavior which predominates during that time when the child is ... detaching himself from the mother and establishing himself as a separate person ... excrement expelled from the body becomes symbolically associated with the ambivalent feelings a child has about separation from his mother and establishment of himself as an autonomous person. Dirt becomes then the recipient of his anger at separation; while love of possessions becomes the substitute for the love of what has been separated from him ... Since racism

involves the separateness of people, so must it become invested with anal fantasies.[16]

In this concept, the black man is associated with the excrement of the anal stage: part of him is hated and becomes the recipient of anger, while part of him becomes revered as a valuable piece of property. But at no time was the black man thought of as possessing human qualities.

Basically, the discussion of the thirteen television seasons and the stereotypes they presented will revolve around the attitudes formulated on these three concepts: (1) the black man as a hated symbol of evil; (2) the black man as a wanton but superior sexual savage "who would screw a snake, if somebody would hold its head!"[17] and (3) the black man as a piece of property to be owned to produce economic wealth. These beliefs caused serious problems to TV producers when they started to present blacks to their audiences.

The television industry was confronted with the problem of representing a minority segment of the population that had been subjected to a great deal of racial hatred. Thus, television needed to balance its sense of social justice and moral obligation with its desire to remain an excellent place to advertise products. In effect, the problem was how to display blacks on TV so they wouldn't threaten or antagonize white viewers and still appease blacks and liberals. The solutions to this problem were examined, season by season, for the major television networks.

---

16 Kovel, 48–49.
17 King, 5.

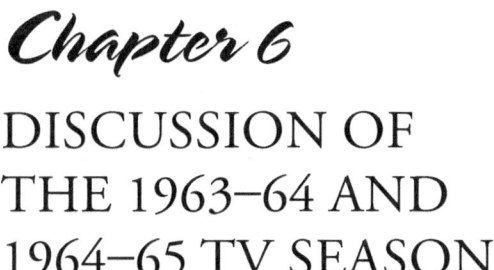

Chapter 6
DISCUSSION OF
THE 1963–64 AND
1964–65 TV SEASONS

Programs with Black Performers: The 1963–64 Season

Fall 1963–64

ABC	CBS	NBC
	East Side/West Side	*Mr. Novak*
		Sing Along with Mitch

Midseason 1963–64

ABC	CBS	NBC
	Jack Benny	*Mr. Novak*
	East Side/West Side	

Programs with Black Performers: The 1964–65 Season

Fall 1964–65

ABC	CBS	NBC
		Mr. Novak
		Jack Benny

Midseason 1964–65

ABC	CBS	NBC
Shindig!*		*Mr. Novak*
		Hullabaloo *

*New this season

The 1963–64 and 1964–65 Television Seasons

In the 1963 and 1964 television seasons, the major networks allotted 3-4 percent of their prime time to programs with at least one black performer. In 1963, ABC had no such programs, but the network improved this situation by allotting 1 percent of prime time to these programs in the 1964–65 season. Conversely, CBS, the perennial programming leader, dropped from 6 percent allotted time in 1963 to 0 percent in 1964–65. This low incidence of network time slotted for programs with black performers indicated the phase that Clark (1972) called non-recognition, in which all minority groups are first subjected to the process of absorption into the dominant group's culture. In the present study, non-recognition was defined under the category of obliteration, which also accounted for the type of portrayals shown on the major networks. Of the six shows aired in 1963–64 and 1964–65 (see Programs with Black Performers, 1963–64 and 1964–65 Seasons), four were variety shows, and the other two depicted a social worker and a schoolteacher.

What is significant in the obliteration category is the implicit assault on the self-concept of the group being obliterated. R. D. Laing (1965) encompasses this process with his concept of "ontological insecurity":

> When he senses his presence in the world as a real, alive, whole and, in a temporal sense, a continuous person … He can go out into the world and meet others: a world and others experienced as equally real, alive, whole and continuous … To the extent that the individual is not reinforced as being real and alive but rather a person who experiences himself as being more dead than alive; precariously differentiated from the rest of the world, so that his identity and autonomy are always in question … He may feel more insubstantial than substantial, and unable to assume that the stuff he is made of is genuine, good and valuable. And he may feel his self as partially divorced from his body. It is, of course, inevitable that an individual whose experience of himself is of this order can no more live in a secure world than he can be secure in himself.[18]

18 R. D. Laing, *The Divided Self* (Baltimore, 1965), 41.

By watching television, which panders to the white viewing audience, blacks subjected themselves to a powerful medium that did not acknowledge their existence as people. Television was reinforcing the concepts of non-recognition and obliteration. Since both children and adults watch a great deal of television, it is particularly distressing to discover that, while white adults and their children were having their existence validated and confirmed, black parents and their children were receiving messages reinforcing their nonexistence or annihilation.

This is not to suggest that television is the determining factor in producing "ontological insecurity" in blacks or other minority groups, but that it can be a contributing factor. By not giving full representation to individuals or groups, television can negatively influence feelings of adequacy in those groups, as well as their capacity to experience themselves as secure and autonomous beings.

Chapter 7
DISCUSSION OF THE 1965–66 AND 1966–67 TV SEASONS

Programs with Black Performers: The 1965–66 Season

Fall 1965–66

ABC	CBS	NBC
Shindig!	*Rawhide*	*Hullabaloo**
*The Long Hot Summer**	*Hogan's Heroes**	*I Spy**
	*The Smothers Brothers Comedy Hour**	

Midseason 1965–66

ABC	CBS	NBC
	*Daktari**	*Hullabaloo*
	Hogan's Heroes	*I Spy*
	The Smothers Brothers Comedy Hour	*The Sammy Davis Jr. Show**

*New this season

Programs with Black Performers: The 1966–67 Season

Fall 1966–67

ABC	CBS	NBC
	Daktari	*I Spy*
	Hogan's Heroes	*Tarzan**
	*Mission: Impossible**	*Star Trek**

Midseason 1965–66

ABC	CBS	NBC
	*Daktari**	*I Spy*

*New this season

The 1965–66 and 1966–67 Television Seasons

In the 1965–66 and 1966–67 seasons, the three major networks increased the prime time allotted to programs with black performers. In the 1965–66 season, the average total prime time was 7 percent; the average total rose to 8 percent during the 1966–67 television season. ABC's allotments rose to 3 percent in 1965–66 but decreased to 0 percent in 1966–67. CBS's were 10 percent and 12 percent during these two seasons, while NBC's were 8 percent and 12 percent. The major networks were increasing their use of black performers during the prime-time hours (Fig. 1), but did the quality of black portrayals also improve?

In 1965–66 and 1966–67, several programs were added to the existing schedules, and a few old programs were cancelled (see Programs with Black Performers, 1965–66 and 1966–67 Seasons). Four of the eight added programs depicted blacks in regulatory roles, three of which could have been played by white actors. Two new programs, *Daktari* and *Tarzan,* used Africa as their locales and employed black actors in subservient roles. The implicit message of these programs seemed to be that, even in the black man's motherland, whites were the dominant, ruling group.

The three most important characters of these years were Scott Alexander, played by Bill Cosby (*I Spy*); Barney, played by Greg Morris (*Mission: Impossible*); and Lieutenant Uhura, played by Nichelle Nichols (*Star Trek*). These characters were important because they appeared on three popular programs that continued to be rerun on smaller networks long after the major networks had canceled the original programs.

Barney (*Mission: Impossible*) was important because, for the first time, blacks saw a strong, athletic figure who was cool under pressure and extremely competent with all types of mechanical and electronic gadgetry. Barney was even allowed to have love affairs in several episodes, but he had no ongoing, steady relations with females. Because Morris was six-foot-four, the writers could have easily made a one-dimensional, strongman character, but fortunately that characterization was given to Greek actor Peter Lupus (strongman and weightlifter).

Scott Alexander (*I Spy*) was cast in a mold similar to Barney's; Alexander was also a secret agent. He was cool and comical but also a master of foreign languages and a Rhodes Scholar. Cosby was originally slated to play a supporting role to the series' star, Robert Culp, but the two actors developed such a good rapport that Culp demanded that Cosby's role be upgraded. During the run of the series, Cosby received three Emmys for his portrayal of Scott Alexander. Like Barney, Scott was allowed to have at least one love affair. Kelly Robinson (Robert Culp), however, was usually involved with a different woman each week. The writers and producers apparently were not afraid of exhibiting the sexuality of their white male lead. Cosby, however, viewed his role differently from what was depicted on television:

> This guy I play likes women—redheads, blondes, all kinds. He's a whole human being. For the first time, a black man sees a woman and wants to make love, to treat her beautifully, the way a woman should be treated by any man. And it's not done like a black man loving a white woman. Just a man,

period. Now how can black people watch only white people make love? That's an illusion wrongly created by Hollywood up to now, and I hope I can change it.[19]

If Cosby filmed any segments with him making love to a white woman, those segments must still be in the "can," because they were never aired on any national network. In fact, only one black was ever allowed to be involved with white women; his name was Cutter (played by Peter De Anda). This was four years after *I Spy* was cancelled at NBC (1972). The TV movie/pilot attempted to capitalize on the great box office success of the movie *Shaft* (which also became a TV series). John Shaft was a hip, sharp-dressing, tough-talking detective who knew no color restrictions when it came to women, and so it was with Frank Cutter.

The *Cutter* pilot was filmed in Chicago, and the plot revolved around Cutter's search for a missing professional quarterback (who was also black). Cutter embodied white male fantasies about blacks: he was a superathlete, he made fools of white males, he disdained "Uncle Tom" blacks, he was sexually free and loved all women, and they (black and white) desired him. Cutter was the star—not somebody's sidekick or subordinate, but his own man. Needless to say, Cutter never became a series; the miracle was that the pilot was aired in the first place. What were NBC producers thinking? True, Cutter had a light complexion, and to that extent, white audiences might have been able to identify him as one of their own. But his orientation and lifestyle were definitely black. Here was an intelligent, socially astute, athletically superior black

---

19 R. Reed, *Do You Sleep in the Nude?* (New York, 1968), 89.

male who loved and was loved by white women. To the extent that the Cutter characterization died a quick death, and that blacks were portrayed as asexual characters to a significant degree, the point was clearly made: network officials would not play upon the fears and fantasies of their major viewing audience because they would lose it. Rather, the network's programming assuaged these fears by portraying blacks as asexual beings who were only rarely allowed to manifest love among themselves.

Lieutenant Uhura (*Star Trek*), a communications officer aboard the starship Enterprise, had an important role: this was the first time a black woman was depicted as something other than a domestic or social worker. Uhura had strong ties to her African heritage; her name means "freedom" in Swahili. She was a respected, competent career woman. However, throughout all Enterprise voyages, Uhura never had any romantic involvement with anyone. For all of her beauty, she was an asexual character; indeed, few black men were on the Enterprise, none with a rank as high as Uhura's. Hopefully, the message of *Star Trek* is not the message from the future: there will be beautiful black women who will be alone due to the nonexistence of capable black men.

Chapter 8
DISCUSSION OF THE 1967–68 AND 1968–69 TV SEASONS

Programs with Black Performers: The 1967–68 Season

Fall 1967–68

ABC	CBS	NBC
Cowboy in Africa*	*Mannix**	*I Spy*
N.Y.P.D.*	*Hogan's Heroes*	*Star Trek*
	Daktari	*Ironside**
	The Smothers Brothers Comedy Hour	*Tarzan*
	Mission: Impossible	

Midseason 1967–68

ABC	CBS	NBC
Cowboy in Africa	Mannix	Rowan & Martin's Laugh-In*
N.Y.P.D.	Hogan's Heroes	I Spy
	The Smothers Brothers Comedy Hour	Ironside
	Mission: Impossible	Tarzan
	Daktari	Star Trek

* New this season

Programs with Black Performers: The 1968–69 Season

Fall 1968–69

ABC	CBS	NBC
Peyton Place	Daktari	Rowan & Martin's Laugh-In
The Outcasts*	Hogan's Heroes	Julia*
The Mod Squad*	Mannix	Ironside*
Land of the Giants*	The Smothers Brothers Comedy Hour	Star Trek
The Felony Squad*	Mission: Impossible	
N.Y.P.D.		

Midseason 1968–69

ABC	CBS	NBC
Peyton Place	*Hogan's Heroes*	*Rowan & Martin's Laugh-In*
The Outcasts	*Mannix*	*Ironside*
The Mod Squad	*The Smothers Brothers Comedy Hour*	*Julia*
N.Y.P.D.	*Mission: Impossible*	*Star Trek*

* New this season

The 1967–68 and 1968–69 Television Seasons

In the 1967–68 and 1968–69 TV seasons, the average total prime-time allotments of programs using black performers rose to 15.6 percent. ABC showed the most dramatic increase by going from zero in 1966–67 to 4 percent and 17 percent in 1967–68 and 1968–69, respectively. CBS increased its black performer representation from 12 percent in 1966–67 to 18 percent in 1967–68 and dropped it slightly to 16 percent in 1968–69. NBC went from 12 percent in 1966–67 to 18 percent in 1967–68 and dipped to 14 percent in 1968–69.

The dramatic rise took place in not only the amount of prime time given to such shows but also the variety of portrayals (Table 2). A bounty hunter, a neurosurgeon, and a rocket ship copilot had joined the list of detectives and secret agents. It was no coincidence that the networks revised their programming in the two seasons after the race riots of 1967, as well as those following the assassination of Rev. Martin Luther King Jr. in 1968. The black ghetto communities of Tampa, Cincinnati, Atlanta, Newark, northern New Jersey, Plainfield, New Brunswick, and Detroit exploded under the weight of the racism and oppression they had suffered for generation after generation. Most whites were frightened and angered by the events of that summer, but most of all they could not understand the motivation behind the riots. Many saw riots as another excuse to loot and rob honest, hardworking white merchants. Others viewed them as the final proof of the innate black stupidity, burning down their own homes. Still others saw these demonstrations of black unrest as proof of the black male's desire to gain power and make love to a white woman.[20] Indeed, this rape fantasy mentioned earlier is often raised in the minds of white racists when blacks demonstrate to gain school integration. Whether the demonstrations are peaceful or violent, the racists' attitudes are the same: they are afraid their daughter or sister might marry one of "them." Hence, any move by blacks to gain a sense of dignity is interpreted as a surreptitious plan to move closer to white women.[21]

On July 29, 1967, President Johnson appointed the National Advisory Commission on Civil Disorders to investigate the 1967 riots and make recommendations for closing the rift between white and black Americans. The commission made this indictment of the mass media complex in the United States:

> They have not communicated to the majority of their audience, which is white, a sense of the degradation, misery, and hopelessness of living in the ghetto. They have not communicated to whites

---

20 Kovel, 72–73.
21 Kovel.

a feeling for the difficulties and frustrations of being a Negro in the United States. They have not shown understanding or appreciation of— and thus have not communicated—a sense of Negro culture, thought or history … If what white America reads in the newspapers or sees on television conditions its expectation of what is ordinary and normal in the larger society, it will neither understand [n]or accept the black American … Television should develop programming which integrates Negroes into all aspects of televised presentations. In addition, we think Negroes should appear more frequently in dramatic and comedy series.[22]

Under such executive pressure, the large increase in programs with black performers is understandable. Since new television programming is scheduled about a year and a half in advance of presentation, the networks tried to comply with the commission's wishes without disturbing their scheduled lineups. Black actors were added to already existing shows or placed in parts written for white actors, which would not lose their "validity" if played by a black actor. The major problem at this time was the paucity of black producers, writers, and directors. The incumbent writers were either guided by stereotypical images or honestly did not know how to create characters who were black and *human*. The easy way out was just to portray blacks as white but without sexuality. Yet to portray blacks in white roles (obliteration) is to lose many positive distinctions between the races; such portrayals strip blacks of their culture and lose them in the milieu of the

22 *Report of the National Advisory Commission on Civil Disorders* (New York: Bantam Books, 1968), 382–386.

society. The networks may have thought they were caught in a double bind: if they portrayed blacks who had sexual interests, they might be accused of perpetuating the "black buck image"; if they showed an individual with no sexual interests, they might be accused of catering to the fears of the white majority. Between these two positions was the argument that television writers are creative people who can use their resources to depict black characters as human without exaggerating their sexual behavior or any other behavior pattern. That this was not done on any consistent or continual basis adds further weight to the idea that fears engendered by the black-rape fantasy directly influenced the black character types finally aired on the networks.

Many new programs key to the image of blacks at that time were aired in 1967–68 and 1968–69: *The Outcasts*, *The Mod Squad*, and *Julia*. More important than the programs were the black characters portrayed on these shows: Jemal David, played by Otis Young (*The Outcasts*); Linc Hayes, played by Clarence Williams III (*The Mod Squad*); and Julia, played by Diahann Carroll (*Julia*).

The Jemal David character had many unusual aspects. It was one of the few roles specifically originated for a black performer, and, though paired with a white costar, he was not a black second banana in the usual sense. In terms of dramatic impact, both stars had equal billing. Each man was an individual trying to survive the best way he knew how. The strength of their relationship was all the more unique when one considers that Jemal's partner, Earl Corey (Don Murray), was an ex-Southern aristocrat and slave owner. To see David assert his rights and express his dignity as an autonomous individual both to Corey and the white environment of the post-Civil War West was an uplifting experience. While Corey and David clearly did not like each other, both came to *respect* one another. It was not an easy matter to keep Young's character operating on a level black audiences could look up to. Offstage, Otis Young constantly battled with scriptwriters to keep from (1) having to degrade other black characters, (2) making his character one-dimensional, and (3) having to shoot other blacks on the series. Due to Young's protests, a black writer was put on the series, but this was a move to appease Young, because, as it turned out, the black writer was powerless to make any significant changes in the series.[23]

That this series never made it into the top ten, lasted only one season, and to this day has not been on any network's rerun schedule suggests that white audiences may, at the very least, have been uncomfortable with the kind of forceful black character Otis Young portrayed.

While Linc Hayes in *The Mod Squad* was not a forceful type like Jemal David, he was identifiably black. He was silent but strong. He wore a dashiki, a large Afro, and shades. His comments were short, perceptive, and to the point. The script/plot depicted Linc as one of three young social outcasts who become undercover cops. Clarence Williams's vast stage experience brought more to his character than did either of his white costars, Michael Cole and Peggy Lipton.

Over the five-year run of the series, Linc was allowed at least two episodes in which he could display his sexuality. Perhaps his

---

23 R. Hobson, "The Odyssey of a Black Man in White Man's Television," *TV Guide*, March 1, 1969, 18–22.

quiet demeanor, asexual behavior and policeman status made him palatable, if not popular, with the mass audience. Clarence Williams III was, however, critical of his role and of black representation on television in general: "All this is escapism, fantasy. This is what the box is all about … The cultural acceptance of black people has not happened yet. The black person's culture has not yet been on TV. Most black parts on TV could be rewritten for whites."[24]

Perhaps *Julia* best represented the high point of fantasy and escapism Williams discussed. In this show a nurse (Diahann Carroll) and her son (Marc Copage) "struggled" to become accepted in a white environment. Julia lived in a beautiful, expensive apartment and dressed lavishly in fashionable clothes. Initially, none of her love interests could measure up to her in values, character, or career goals. For the first two seasons, the most dominant male figure in her life was her son. It was interesting that a "boy" held this position of importance. When an adult black male is called "boy," it is an insult. The connotation of the word *boy* suggests a lack of autonomy and sexual maturity, hence a nonexistent sexual threat.

Here the black male image was depicted as a sexually immature boy who mumbled most of his lines. Such a program was covertly degrading to blacks but not threatening to white viewers. In the last season of *Julia*, the producers took a chance and introduced a black lawyer (ex-football star Fred Williamson) to provide a love interest, but the move was too late to affect the impact of the show's established format.

Most viewers could swallow the candy-coated *Julia* as easily as a Life Saver. Wasn't the character of Julia the ideal blacks were

---

24 J. Riley, "How I Feel about Being Black," *TV Guide*, February 28, 1970, 20–22.

striving to emulate? Perhaps, but the show didn't represent what most blacks were like; it was simply more pabulum for whites while being mildly entertaining to blacks. On the positive side, *Julia* was one of the few shows with a black star but no white costar to offset her impact, except maybe Julia herself.

The Outcasts, *The Mod Squad*, and *Julia* were three different approaches the major networks employed in their attempt to comply with the riot commission's mandate and still attract a broad viewership.

Chapter 9
DISCUSSION OF THE 1969–70 AND 1970–71 TV SEASONS

Programs with Black Performers: The 1969–70 Season

Fall 1969–70

ABC	CBS	NBC
Love, American Style*	Hogan's Heroes	Rowan & Martin's Laugh-In
The New People*	Mannix	Julia*
The Mod Squad*	The Leslie Uggams Show	Daniel Boone*
Room 222*	Mission: Impossible	Ironside
Land of the Giants		The Bill Cosby Show*

Midseason 1969–70

ABC	CBS	NBC
Room 222	Mannix	The Bill Cosby Show
The Mod Squad	Mission: Impossible	Ironside
Land of the Giants	Hogan's Heroes	Daniel Boone
Love, American Style		The Protectors*

* New this season

Programs with Black Performers: The 1970–71 Season

Fall 1970–71

ABC	CBS	NBC
Monday Night Football	The Interns*	Rowan & Martin's Laugh-In
The Young Lawyers*	Mission: Impossible	Julia
The Mod Squad	Mannix	The Flip Wilson Show*
Dan August*	Hogan's Heroes	Ironside
Barefoot in the Park*	Storefront Lawyers*	McCloud*
The Young Rebels*		The Protectors
The Silent Force*		
Matt Lincoln*		
Love, American Style*		
Make Room for Granddaddy*		

* New this season

Midseason 1970–71

Fall 1970–71

ABC	CBS	NBC
The Mod Squad	All in the Family	Rowan & Martin's Laugh-In
Room 222	Mannix	Julia
The Young Lawyers	The Interns	The Flip Wilson Show
Dan August	Mission: Impossible	The Bill Cosby Show
Love, American Style	Hogan's Heroes	The Protectors
The Pearl Bailey Show*	Storefront Lawyers	McCloud
Make Room for Granddaddy		

* New this season

The 1969–70 and 1970–71 Television Seasons

During the 1969–70 and 1970–71 seasons, the number of prime-time programs with black performers reached its peak. ABC's prime-time allotment dropped to 15 percent in 1969–70 but rose to a high of 28 percent in 1970–71. CBS and NBC went from 12 percent and 15 percent respectively in 1969–70 to 19 percent each in 1970–71. All three networks devoted an average of 22 percent of their prime-time hours to shows with black performers.

A larger variety of roles played by black actors surfaced as well. At no other time were blacks (male and female) represented in such a great number of positive career role models (Table 4). Of the many new programs of these two seasons, the most notable were *Room 222*, *The Bill Cosby Show*, *The Flip Wilson Show*, *All in the Family*, and *Monday Night Football*.

After his previous success in *I Spy* (see 1965–66 TV season), Bill Cosby returned to television in a half-hour comedy in which he played a physical education teacher, Chet Kincaid. Unlike his previous series, Cosby was the star. The program, at best, was only mildly entertaining and could not be ranked with Cosby's better efforts, but it was significant in the way Cosby insisted upon the use and training of blacks in all production aspects of his show, behind as well as before the camera. For this reason alone, the show is a landmark in television broadcasting.

Perhaps the show that incorporated all of the best images for blacks was *Room 222*. For a half-hour each week, audiences saw a competent, intelligent, black male American history teacher and an equally competent, beautiful black guidance counselor discharge their professional duties with warmth and acumen. They related to their students (black and white) and professional staff as multidimensional characters. This was also one of the few shows in which blacks had an ongoing relationship that treated each individual with love and respect. The show worked. It avoided all negative stereotypes, ran for five seasons (ABC), and was later picked up for daytime reruns by another major network (NBC).

Did this mean the producers would no longer be afraid to show blacks as complete characters? Would there be a rush of programs to capitalize on the success of *Room 222*? One night of viewing the programs of 1975–76 or the subsequent sections of this study will reveal the answer. Part of it could be found in one of the most popular shows of 1970–71, *The Flip Wilson Show*. To understand this show's appeal, one need look no further than Wilson's engaging characters. Perhaps Les Brown (1971) said it best:

> Why did Wilson catch on? … First, because he had never been a second banana and could conduct a show of his own without seeming out of character. Second, because his source of humor was not white society but black, and in that sense it was original for television, other Negroes in the medium having had to pretend the races had a common culture. Third, he was a one-man repertory company, having developed two characters outside his own stand-up identity, the Reverend Leroy of the Church of What's Happening Now and Harlem chatterbox Geraldine Jones. Both were satirical types and so distinctly Negro they had no credible coordinates in white society. Fourth, his comedy was not an ethnic argument; rather than sentimentalizing Negro-American culture, it seemed to mock it. And fifth, it did mock it.[25]

For a black man to dress in drag to humorously debase the black female image implies several negative stereotypes: (1) the black man is a castrated figure who desires to become a woman so he may better assert himself, and (2) the black female is an unattractive masculine figure who dotes on sex. In addition, some of the most important leaders of black movements (ministers)

---

25 L. Brown, *Television: The Business Behind the Box* (New York, 1971), 150.

are really charlatans who deceive their naive followers into giving them money to buy Cadillacs or other expensive luxuries. That Wilson was simultaneously funny and degrading made his show doubly insidious. Blacks watched Wilson and enjoyed his witty perceptions on some obscure aspects of black ghetto culture, and whites enjoyed him because he confirmed beliefs they had about blacks. They were also comforted by the notion that the black sexual superman they feared was really only a transvestite or a sexually ambiguous individual.

When a program like *The Flip Wilson Show* can premier the season after *Room 222*, this definitely shows that, for all their progress, the networks were still not ready to deal seriously with the problem of presenting viable black images. Perhaps even more insidious than *The Flip Wilson Show* was the ABC network's decision to present NFL football during the prime-time hours. Anyone familiar with professional football is also aware of the image football projects in terms of the athlete, particularly black athletes. Professional football is a prime example of how pro sports treat athletes like property. The concept of dehumanization or thingification is dramatically displayed in organized professional football.

Meggyesy (1970), Edwards (1970), Paris (1971), Shaw (1972), and Allsopp (1974) have graphically sketched the history of the feudal lord-serf relationship once prevalent in professional and amateur sports. But even within the serf's realm, white serfs (athletes) have always felt superior to black serfs (athletes). When athletes are considered commodities, the best buy on the market is the black athlete. Because they were not sophisticated in contract negotiations, black athletes were duped into signing contracts below the salary scales of comparable white athletes. In fact, the NFL employed former black running back Buddy Young to go to the homes of prospective black athletes and convince their parents of the NFL's sincerity and the fruitlessness of acquiring a business agent. For his efforts, Mr. Young received 10 percent of what the league figured he saved them by beating down young players on their contracts.[26] In return, pro football expected their black athletes to (1) play when injured, since blacks' thresholds of pain were higher than whites; (2) perform in an errorless, machinelike manner; (3) never become tired; (4) adopt a subordinate attitude; and (5) accept insults and racial ridicule.

Black ballplayers are selected even more stringently on the basis of "correct attitude" than whites. Blacks are in an especially difficult position. If they act like Toms, they will be dominated by white ballplayers and lose respect for themselves and each other. But if they are too "militant" and try to assert their basic manhood by trying to break out of the white's stereotype of the shuffling, dumb, insensitive jock, they are immediately under suspicion and cut from the squad.[27]

A case in point was Edward McQuarters of Oklahoma University, who was cut from the St. Louis Cardinals because of attitude. McQuarters had the temerity to show respect for his black teammates. He refused to smile at jokes pertaining to blacks' inherent ability to run fast or their "known" insensitivity to pain, and he refused to be insulted by any player without retaliating in kind.[28] McQuarters was thus rebelling against the entire notion of

---

26 B. Parrish, *They Call It a Game* (New York, 1971), 150.
27 D. Meggyesy, *Out of Their League* (California, 1970), 195.
28 Loc, cit.

thingification—the idea that he, as a black athlete, was a machine, a piece of property to be used or abused at white society's leisure. Asserting his humanity ran counter to whites' deeply set attitudes about blacks. Had McQuarters been permitted to continue, his behavior would have not only been detrimental to the Cardinals and the professional sports complex, but it also would have threatened the dominant-subordinate relationship between blacks and whites. Because professional football could not afford to project such an image to its fans, McQuarters and those like him had to go.

White professional football players were really no different from white males in general when it came to the black-rape fantasy:

> The real problem is that white football players feel blacks always want to jump in the sack with their wives or any white woman they see on the street. "You white guys ask any of us here who we like, and I'm sure to the man, every black football player will say he prefers black women … That's the reason why you guys get upset because you think we want to screw every white woman we see." The squirming throughout the room indicated that Edwards had indeed struck one of the most sensitive nerves of white football players' racism.[29]

Perhaps the most insidious stereotype indigenous to football is the myth of the black quarterback—a myth because the twenty-eight professional teams have virtually no black quarterbacks (except for Jim Plunkett of San Francisco, Joe Gilliam of New

---

29 Meggyesy, 219.

Orleans, and James Harris of San Diego). Not allowing blacks to play quarterback is closely tied to the thingification concept whites have about blacks. The connotation of being a quarterback is that one has (1) intelligence, (2) leadership qualities, and (3) a good passing arm.

Professional football coaches, either influenced by their readings of Dr. Jensen and Dr. Shockley (in reference to the low IQ potential of blacks) or their acquired attitudes, believe black athletes are not equipped to handle the "thinking" positions of quarterback, guard, or center. There has even been conjecture that blacks' arms are hinged differently at the shoulder, making it difficult for them to achieve the proper throwing motion, but that this "flaw" is compensated for by their generally larger buttocks, which allow them to excel at positions requiring quick and fluid movements.[30]

Aside from the questionable validity of these notions, none really have to do with a coach's decision not to use blacks at the quarterback position. It is, rather, the unsettling idea of having a black in a leadership position, giving orders and directions to whites, particularly before national television audiences. In addition, a black as quarterback plays havoc with the fantasies of whites who project themselves into the quarterback position, giving them the powerful sensation of not only directing other whites but also a slave owner's omnipotence in controlling his flock of black savages. The allegation is that Joe Gilliam was removed from his starting position with the Pittsburgh Steelers (1974–75 season) precisely because the fans could not reconcile their fantasies by having a black at the helm of leadership. Gilliam's

---

30 G. Halsell, *Black and White Sex* (New York, 1972), 41.

removal came even though he had performed competently, and at the time of his demotion his team had a winning record.

Monday Night Football, via the absence of blacks from the "thinking" positions, reinforced the stereotype of subhuman, unintelligent, machinelike characteristics of the black male. Thus, the decision to put pro football on prime-time television amplified the reality of racist stereotypes, rather than serving as a balm to soothe the tensions between blacks and whites in compliance with the riot commission's suggestions.

Another important show of the 1970–71 season was *All in the Family*. Its main character, Archie Bunker, played superbly by Carroll O'Connor, was a working-class bigot who was ignorant and boisterous in his denouncement of everything liberal. He dealt with every racial group in terms of their "popular" stereotypes, but in a humorous way. Due to the great acting skill of O'Connor, who made the character a sympathetic one, the show enjoyed great popularity. Unfortunately, many people who watched the show agreed with Bunker's point of view: he was not a caricature to them but a reinforcement of their own attitudes about minority groups.

Most of all, the show, through its use of unique character types, launched such spin-off shows as *Maude*, *Good Times*, and *The Jeffersons*, which also presented stereotyped views of blacks. Still, with all of the allegations about the shows of 1969–70 and 1970–71, they were the best in terms of the number of programs that included blacks and the great variety of roles blacks were permitted to play.

Chapter 10
DISCUSSION OF THE 1971–72 AND 1972–73 TV SEASONS

Programs with Black Performers: The 1971–72 Season

Fall 1971–72

ABC	CBS	NBC
Monday Night Football	Mannix	Rowan & Martin's Laugh-In
The Mod Squad	Mission: Impossible	McCloud
Love, American Style	All in the Family	Ironside
Room 222		The Flip Wilson Show
		The Bold Ones
		The Partners*
		The Funny Side*

Midseason 1971–72

ABC	CBS	NBC
The Mod Squad	Mannix	Rowan & Martin's Laugh-In
Kopykats*	All in the Family	The Flip Wilson Show
Room 222	Mission: Impossible	Ironside
Love, American Style		Sanford and Son*
		Emergency*
		The Bold Ones
		McCloud

* New this season

Programs with Black Performers: The 1972–73 Season

Fall 1972–73

ABC	CBS	NBC
Monday Night Football	The New Bill Cosby Show*	Rowan & Martin's Laugh-In
The Rookies*	Mannix	The Bold Ones
Room 222	Maude*	Emergency
Temperatures Rising*	All in the Family	The Flip Wilson Show
The Streets of San Francisco*	Mission: Impossible	Ironside
Love, American Style		McCloud
The Mod Squad		Sanford and Son

Midseason 1972–73

ABC	CBS	NBC
The Rookies	The New Bill Cosby Show	Rowan & Martin's Laugh-In
Temperatures Rising	Mannix	The Flip Wilson Show
The Mod Squad	Maude	Ironside
Room 222	Mission: Impossible	Sanford and Son
The Streets of San Francisco	All in the Family	Emergency
		McCloud

* New this season

The 1971–72 and 1972–73 Television Seasons

In the 1971–72 and 1972–73 seasons, the number of prime-time hours allotted to programs with black performers began to decline slightly, 16 percent in 1971–72, but then they increased to 20 percent in 1972–73. ABC's allotment dropped to 16 percent in 1971–72 and then increased to 24 percent in 1972–73. CBS's allotments also declined to 12 percent in 1971–72 and to 16 percent in 1972–73. NBC's allotment rose, however, during these two seasons to 20 percent and 21 percent in 1971–72 and 1972–73, respectively. The most notable shows of these two seasons were *Sanford and Son* and *Tenafly*.

The popularity of Fred Sanford (Redd Foxx) and Lamont Sanford (Demond Wilson) was unquestionable. It was a funny, entertaining show, full of all of the negative stereotypes blacks have been trying to eradicate. In a large sense, it was a modern-day *Amos 'n Andy* (a detrimental comedy show about blacks the NAACP finally succeeded in pressuring CBS to take off the air in the late 1950s). *Sanford and Son*, based on an English comedy called *Steptoe and Son*, was written to encompass the nuances of black ghetto culture and, to that extent, give an index to what whites thought ghetto black was really like. According to the images the show projected, blacks were (1) dishonest in their dealings with one another, (2) big drinkers, (3) possessive and deceitful with one another in their family interactions, (4) disrespectful in their verbal interactions between males and females, (5) in the company of a prevalent number of unattractive black females, (6) lazy and shiftless, (7) generally biased against whites and Hispanics, and (8) incapable of maintaining ongoing relationships with the opposite sex.[31]

Despite these allegations, *Sanford and Son* was a popular show, basically for the same reasons that blacks and whites supported *The Flip Wilson Show* (see 1970–71 season).

Tenafly was a black detective who, unlike his predecessors, was just your ordinary, middle-class family man trying to make a living. James McEachin played the role in such an honest, warm fashion that the character had a ring of truth about him, and the show was not offensive to anyone. Tenafly did require a great deal of thinking for the writers as well as viewers. After being conditioned to think all black detectives would be superintelligent, action-oriented, and basically asexual characters, the audience saw an unflamboyant type who punched a time clock and was greatly concerned about his family, the traffic, getting to work, and the

---

31 E. Collier, "Sanford and Son Is White to the Core," *New York Times*, July 1, 1973, 1.

menacing crabgrass on his front lawn.

Perhaps *Tenafly* was too ambitious in its pronouncements of middle-class values, but it was the only program of its genre to show (1) an intact family grouping with the black male as its leader, (2) honest and warm interaction within the black family group, (3) emphasis on the sensitive and human qualities of its black characters, and (4) family problems dealt with seriously, not comically.

Curiously enough, both *Tenafly* and *Sanford and Son* were produced for the same network (NBC). One can speculate about the network's intentions of achieving a balanced representation of blacks by having two such divergent shows, but, as the following seasons revealed, the format of *Sanford and Son*, not *Tenafly*, would set the pattern for presenting black family interactions.

Chapter 11
DISCUSSION OF THE 1973–74 TV SEASON

Programs with Black Performers: The 1973–74 Season

Fall 1973–74

ABC	CBS	NBC
Monday Night Football	*Maude*	*The Magician**
Temperatures Rising	*Shaft**	*The Flip Wilson Show*
Love, American Style	*Mannix*	*Ironside*
*Love Thy Neighbor**	*Roll Out**	*Sanford and Son*
*The Streets of San Francisco**	*All in the Family*	*Emergency*
The Rookies	*Calucci's Department*	*McCloud*

Room 222

Ozzie's Girls*

Midseason 1973–74

ABC	**CBS**	**NBC**
The Rookies	*Shaft*	*Tenafly*
The Cowboys*	*Mannix*	*The Flip Wilson Show*
Firehouse*	*All in the Family*	*Sanford and Son*
Love, American Style	*Good Times**	*Ironside*
The Streets of San Francisco		*Emergency*
		McCloud

---

* New this season

The 1973–74 Television Season

During the 1973–74 season, the major networks' allotment of prime-time hours for programs with black performers remained high, yet declined from the previous season. ABC decreased its allotments from 24 to 21 percent. CBS lowered its allotments from 16 to 14 percent. NBC went from 21 to 18.5 percent. The landmark shows this season were *Shaft, Roll Out, Love Thy Neighbor,* and *Good Times.*

Roll Out was loosely based on the exploits of the Red Ball Express of World War II, whose drivers were black. Ostensibly, the idea of accounting for the historical existence of the Red Ball Express would be a valuable addition to defining the blacks' contribution to this country's war effort. However, the notion that blacks had to be separated from whites because of their alleged lack of courage and low scores on army classification tests was grounded in the psychodynamic matrix of anality (thingification) and sexuality: (1) if blacks inherently lacked courage and could be frightened as easily as little children, then indeed they *were* children and not to be considered a sexual threat to the white woman; and (2) since blacks are subhuman, they cannot possess average or superior intelligence. It was on the basis of these two racist assumptions that the Quarter Master Corps, the Corps of Engineers, and the Transportation Corps accounted for more than 67 percent of the black enlisted men in World War II.[32] To present a program in which blacks in the Transportation Corps engage in humorous activities and prankish behavior could only serve to reinforce the rationale on which this segregated unit was organized.

Roll Out was supposed to be a black spin-off of the popular movie and TV series *M*A*S*H*. The critical difference was that, in *M*A*S*H*, the pranksters were medical officers who could command respect when necessary. In contrast, in *Roll Out* the pranksters and goof-offs were the lowly black privates and enlisted men disciplined by white commissioned officers or their overseers. Generally, the discipline was zealously administered through a black sergeant (Mel Stewart) who, subservient to his white superior officers, showed no compassion in his treatment of the black enlisted men. Indeed, such a situation recalled the overseer status given to certain "good" slaves to make their

---

32 E. Daviney, R. Star, E. Suchman, and S. Stouffer, eds., *The American Soldier: Adjustment During Army Life* (Princeton, NJ: Princeton University Press, 1949), 530.

brethren more productive. So grateful were these overseers to be closely identified with their white masters' position of power that they were more cruel and ruthless than any white overseer could be.

In *Roll Out*, the general attitude was that the enlisted men were like children (mischievous but sexually immature) who had to be constantly watched and disciplined. The soldiers, in turn, had no recourse but to act out their resentments on each other. Their pranks and generally deceitful behavior supplied the show's humorous aspect. In effect, the image of the show tended to (1) degrade the reputation of the Red Ball Express, (2) reinforce the idea that blacks were childlike and unintelligent, (3) suggest that interactions among blacks were basically deceitful, and (4) comically depict the slave-master relationship between the officers and enlisted men.

In the same season, ABC aired a show for only five weeks that concerned a black couple moving into an all-white neighborhood and their interactions with the whites next door: *Love Thy Neighbor*. Janet MacLachlan and Harrison Page were cast as the black couple. MacLachlan portrayed an attractive, calm, socially conscious black woman, but Page played an excitable, childlike black male eager to conform to white society standards. Except for his color, Page's character was not identifiably black, but a caricature of what a middle-class black male was supposed to be like: well-educated, neatly dressed, attentive to proper speech and behavior, indifferent to his wife's sexuality. By contrast, his next-door neighbor was a young, ignorant Archie Bunker-type (see *All in the Family*). His neighbor's one advantage was that he was white, and through various means he never let Ferguson Bruce (Page) forget this essential difference. Throughout the five shows, every black stereotype from sex and intelligence to athletic ability was dredged up by the neighbor (Ron Masak) in his attempt to become better acquainted with the Bruces.

The image projected was one of the black male (1) rejecting his culture; (2) adopting white, middle-class values; (3) acting in a hysterical, childlike manner; and (4) de-emphasizing his closeness to his wife. The *coup de grace* was that Ferguson found that, no matter how he progressed, he would never be accepted as a white man, but only as a buffoon to be ridiculed and laughed at.

A character no one laughed at was John Shaft. *Shaft* was another attempt by CBS to make a hit movie into a popular TV series vis-à-vis *M*A*S*H*. In the movie, John Shaft was a black James Bond noted for his rapier-like insults, leather wardrobe, machismo, and fantasy-like lovemaking with women of different races.[33] The *Shaft* movie had wide box-office appeal to both black and white moviegoers. Before the series, CBS had run the movie on its *Friday Night Movie* and subsequently decided that *Shaft* and the *Shaft* theme song (which sold over a million copies) were enough to guarantee a successful series.

The series, however, was a dismal failure. Why? Precisely because the only recognizable aspect of *Shaft* was the music and actor Richard Roundtree. Gone were the character's swagger and sharp insults (which were adaptations of what ghetto residents call "playing the dozens"), and most of all, TV's John Shaft had lost his sexuality, stripped of his women and superstud love scenes;

---

33 C. Riley, "A Black Movie for White Audiences?" *New York Times*, July 25, 1971, 13.

essentially he had become an asexual white detective in blackface. The TV writers of *Shaft*, Allen Balter and William Read, explained what they were told to do:

> Our job was to make all America accept a black leading man. We were conscious of the image of Shaft in film and deliberately worked against it in our show. Everyone agreed from the start, Shaft had to win and keep a broad cross-section of the audience. We knew we'd get bad reviews but we thought the American public would accept this man as their friend.[34]

It is a laudable endeavor to have a black leading man on a ninety-minute prime-time show that is dramatic in nature. The restructuring of the John Shaft character, however, underscored the extremes to which television would go to make a black character palatable to its major commodity-buying audience. Perhaps fearful that *Shaft* would have a fate similar to the pilot for *Cutter* (see 1965–66 and 1966–67 seasons), CBS decided to de-emphasize the "soul" in John Shaft. It was damaging enough to the self-concept of blacks to see themselves represented as one-dimensional, asexual characters, but to take an established black folk hero and whiten, brighten and castrate him for the purpose of selling laundry detergents and underarm deodorants was devastating. The network's concern was not to show a character that would enable blacks to fantasize about having autonomy and power but to assure whites that Shaft was just another harmless black man, working within the system and wanting more than

---

34 B. Adler, "You Can't Put That Shaft on TV," *TV Guide*, April 20, 1973, 27.

anything to be their friend.

In 1973–74, CBS aired another show about blacks: *Good Times*. The lead character was a maid called Florida (played by Esther Rolle) who used to work for Maude (see *All in the Family*, 1970–71 season). Florida lived in a Chicago tenement with her family, who were poor but proud and seemingly having "good times." Several inescapable stereotypes were evident during each segment: (1) the ineffectual father (while he commanded respect in the family, he couldn't stay employed long enough to provide for them); (2) generally insulting interactions between brother and sister; (3) the black female image as an unattractive mammy; (4) the use of slang as a means of communication; (5) the suggestion that blacks considered each other ugly; and (6) the implication that the socially militant and heritage-conscious black was really a little boy (projected by having the smallest, youngest member of the family express these views).

What kept *Good Times* on the air was that both whites and blacks found it entertaining, and of course, it presented nonthreatening images to whites. It was the formula for an acceptable show, in which both blacks and whites could laugh at the antics of other blacks. TV producers believed whites could comfortably watch any show that portrayed blacks as childlike (not sexually threatening), living in abject poverty away from whites, and not accusing them as the cause of their circumstances.

Presenting blacks in sitcoms based on the *Good Times* format would eventually become the trend for putting a greater number of blacks on television. A negative trend, which did not consider black families as serious entities and conveyed many of the derogatory ideas whites had about black family life, became dominant.

Perhaps one might think too much is being made over stereotyping and misrepresenting the black family because the medium of television basically distorts everything, without preference to race. One need only examine such white family shows of the past and present to know that great care was taken to make these shows sensitive, perceptive portrayals of white family life. These shows include *Mama* (based on the 1944 John Van Druten play and 1948 film adaptation *I Remember Mama*), *Life with Father*, *Ozzie and Harriet*, *The Brady Bunch*, *The Waltons*, and *The Family*.

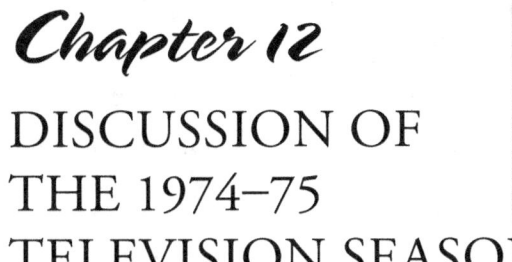

Chapter 12
DISCUSSION OF THE 1974–75 TELEVISION SEASON

Programs with Black Performers: The 1974–75 Season

Fall 1974–75

ABC	CBS	NBC
Monday Night Football	Good Times	Ironside
The Streets of San Francisco	Mannix	Sanford and Son
The Rookies	All in the Family	Emergency
Get Christie Love*		Chico and the Man*
That's My Mama*		Police Woman*
		McCloud

Midseason 1972–73

ABC	CBS	NBC
The Rookies	Good Times	Sanford and Son
The Streets of San Francisco	Tony Orlando and Dawn*	Chico and the Man
S.W.A.T.*	The Jeffersons*	Emergency
Caribe*	Mannix	Police Woman
That's My Mama		McCloud
Get Christie Love		
Hot L Baltimore		
Baretta *		
Barney Miller*		

* New this season

The 1974–75 Television Season

In the 1974–75 season, the amount of prime-time hours allotted to programs with black performers declined to an average total of 16.5 percent of the combined seventy-five hours available to the major networks. ABC increased its allotment from 21 percent in 1973 to 24 percent in this season. CBS cut back its allotments from 14 to 10 percent, as did NBC, from 18.5 to 15.5 percent. Despite the slight decrease in the prime-time hours allotted, the total number of programs with black performers and the amount of television exposure given to blacks was almost what they received before the civil disturbances and the mandate of the president's commission. As we have seen, however, greater exposure does not necessarily imply representations of high quality.

This season saw a rush of new programs using black actors (see 1974–75 season). Some of the most popular were *Get Christie Love*, *That's My Mama*, *Baretta*, and *The Jeffersons*.

Get Christie Love starred Teresa Graves, who had been a regular on the 1969-70 season of *Rowan and Martin's Laugh-In*, as a police detective. Christie Love was black, sexy, and independent, as well as a karate expert. According to her captain, she was "the best *man* I have on the force." In short, Christie Love was superwoman; even more, she was as good as a man. To imply that a woman can function just like a man is to strip her of her femininity and, perhaps, suggest that she might be more masculine than feminine. Surely Christie Love tried to maintain her status as a woman by wearing attractive clothes, but when she engaged in shoot-outs and fist-fights with males, the femininity in her image was strained.

In the early segments, Christie had no men in her life, save her police partner. She was not interacting with any black males on any personal or meaningful basis. By contrast, NBC aired the series *Police Woman* in the same season, starring Angie Dickinson as Pepper. Though Pepper engaged in police activities, she was allowed to keep her femininity. Her male partner assumed the physical burdens of the job. Pepper was not a loner or a show-off who had to prove herself the equal of any man.

As Teresa Graves became more involved in Bible study, she requested that her character be rewritten to take out the violence and sexual inferences. A feminine, less violent, less vulgar, more vulnerable Christie Love was not what the TV audience wanted to see, and the show's ratings dropped; the major viewing audience would apparently not accept an attractive black woman as anything less than an aggressive, sexy female on whom they might project their sexual fantasies.

Once the sexy-aggressive image had been created, the viewing public would not accept Christie Love as simply a woman, nor would they permit Pepper to be anything less than a woman. Pepper, as a white woman, was on a pedestal with her femininity assured and her pureness protected. *Get Christie Love* and *Police Woman* exemplify the old notions of the pure white female and sensual black female perpetuated as standard fare on major network television.

The other well-known black female stereotype is the nurturing old mammy. This image was on display on ABC's *That's My Mama*. Theresa Merritt played Mrs. Curtis, matriarch of the Curtis family. Her son, Clifton Curtis (played by Clifton Davis), ran the family barbershop and ran after women. But Mrs. Curtis (a widow) seemed determined to keep her son from leading his own life, and Clifton was unable to cut his umbilical ties to his mother.

The series was complete with blacks scheming to get ahead, loud dressing/slang-talking characters, and a middle-class black so estranged from his culture he sounded like a white man trying to be black. All of these characters were in some way influenced and warmly dominated by Mrs. Curtis. This was a family comedy with a mammy type as the most dominant, sensible and understanding of any of the other male or female characters. This may have been the black family the way whites envisioned it, but it did not represent all black families. In this sense, it is degrading to present black families in ways that conform to popular stereotypes, rather than giving the audience insights into other strong, patriarchal black families.

The Jeffersons depicted an intact family unit, yet the "man" of the house was flawed in several key ways: (1) he was racist in his views about whites; (2) he believed in using deceit to get ahead in the world; (3) he constantly argued with and yelled at his wife; (4) he was short, making his temper tantrums appear like the outbursts of a small child; (5) his wife was a heavy-set mammy type; and (6) his mother dominated him. For all of his racist comments, George Jefferson (played by Sherman Helmsley) was presented as an innocuous little mouse (much like the youngest son on *Good Times*, who was more amusing than threatening to the viewing audience). In fact, George believed many of the same ideas whites did, e.g., that there should be no mixed marriages. He constantly insulted both partners of a mixed marriage, thus representing the majority of whites on this issue.

Although having a mixed couple on a prime-time show was a major step for television, the producer stayed within the tabooed limits. Had the couple been a black male and white female, the show would likely not have lasted two weeks. Not only did a white male/black female couple fulfill certain white male fantasies about the desirability of the black female, but most interracial relationships have historically taken place between white males and black females. In addition, the show's only attractive females were Roxie Roker (who played the wife in the mixed couple) and her daughter (the product of a mixed marriage), suggesting that the white male was capable of appreciating, responding to, and producing attractive, independent, black women.

In the season's final new show, *Baretta* actor Robert Blake was sometimes assisted by a slang-talking, colorful-dressing pimp known as "the Rooster" (played by Michael D. Roberts), which marked the first time a black could fully explore his sexual nature on a show. To be human, one must possess sexuality, but solely possessing sexuality does not make a character human. Instead of presenting the usual asexual type, this program went to the other extreme: showing a black man who treated sex as a business. The Rooster had both white and black girls in his stable, which implied that he provided both love and protection to all his girls and perhaps was not opposed to bringing underage white girls into his fold.

One purpose of this study is to emphasize that most black characters are hyposexual because the TV industry does not want to intimidate or scare away the white audience (which buys most of the advertised products). Consequently, blacks are usually represented as one-dimensional, completely devoid of sexuality. The idea proposed is to have more multidimensional characters rooted in the black experience. It is not a remedy to have another unidimensional character whose proclivity happens to be sexual exploitation.

The Rooster was comical and, as such, might not have been a threatening image to whites. But he did conform to the idea of the sexually aggressive black male and the black-rape fantasy. In addition, the Rooster was a poor role model for blacks. A pimp simply cannot uplift blacks' sense of importance in this society, nor did he represent what blacks felt about sex and white women.

The advent of the black male as pimp and sociopath began with the 1974–75 season but would continue to grow and fester in 1975–76.

Chapter 13
DISCUSSION OF THE 1975–76 TV SEASON

Programs with Black Performers: The 1975–76 Season

Fall 1975–76

ABC	CBS	NBC
Monday Night Football	Beacon Hill*	Joe Forrester*
The Streets of San Francisco	Tony Orlando and Dawn	Sanford and Son
The Rookies	The Jeffersons	Chico and the Man
That's My Mama	Good Times	Emergency
Baretta	Bronk*	Police Woman*
Starsky & Hutch*		Grady*
On the Rocks*		The Cop & the Kid*
S.W.A.T.		McCloud

Barney Miller
*Welcome Back, Kotter**

Midseason 1975–76

ABC	CBS	NBC
The Streets of San Francisco	*Tony Orlando and Dawn*	*Joe Forrester*
Welcome Back, Kotter	*Bronk*	*McCloud*
Baretta	*The Jeffersons**	*Sanford and Son*
Starsky & Hutch	*Good Times*	*Chico and the Man*

---

* New this season

Midseason 1975–76

ABC	CBS	NBC
S.W.A.T.		*Emergency*
On the Rocks		*Police Woman*
Barney Miller		
The Rookies		

The 1975–76 Television Season

In 1975–76, the amount of prime-time hours allotted to programs with black performers increased to an average total of 21.6 percent for the major networks. ABC's representation rose from 24 to 31 percent. CBS increased its prime-time allotments from 10 to

14 percent, while NBC went from 15.5 to 20 percent. The 21.6 percent figure was the highest number of prime-time hours given to programs with black performers since the 22 percent figure of 1970–71.

It has been stated that the 1970–71 season was important because blacks played a great variety of roles, and in one show (*Room 222*) they were treated as multidimensional characters and presented as positive role models. The 1975–76 season, however, failed to respond to the needs of blacks and whites by continuing to show the negative stereotypes of the previous season (Table 3).

Joining *Sanford and Son*, *That's My Mama*, *Baretta*, *The Jeffersons*, and *Good Times* were such programs as *Beacon Hill*; *Welcome Back, Kotter*; *Starsky & Hutch*; *On the Rocks*; *Joe Forrester*; *Grady*; *The Cop and the Kid*; *Bronk*; and a summer pilot called *What's Happening!!*

Joe Forrester had another black pimp (played by James A. Watson Jr.), who often made the perfect fall guy for Forrester (Lloyd Bridges). This pimp either solicited runaway teenage girls (usually white) for prostitution or had the inside scoop on some criminal activity. In addition to the Rooster on *Baretta*, *Joe Forrester* presented too many negative stereotypes about black males, in both sexual aspirations toward white women and their proclivity for criminality.

Starsky & Hutch and *On the Rocks* brought more criminal types to the prime-time TV audience. Huggy Bear (Antonio Fargas) owned a bar in the ghetto. The bar was a haven for several criminal types he knew personally. One got the impression that Huggy had been in prison but was trying to reform. Starsky and Hutch frequently visited Huggy's bar to get information about that week's crime. The program tried to balance the character of Huggy by having a black police captain (played by Bernie Hamilton), who was only black by accident of his color and not by the character he portrayed.

On the Rocks concerned convicts in a minimum-security prison. All of the heroes were convicted felons living in the same cellblock, which was racially integrated, with two whites, one Hispanic and one black prisoner (Hal Williams). The prison-guard cadre was also integrated, with one white (Tom Poston) and one black (Mel Stewart).

Comparisons have been made between the prisons and the Old South's slavery system by former boxer Rubin Carter, and between slavery and the segregated black units of World War II by this writer. Interestingly, Mel Stewart, who played the overseer-type sergeant in *Roll Out*, was called to duplicate his role as an overseer-type prison guard in *On the Rocks*. Again, Stewart's character was subservient to the warden and extremely strict and vindictive with the prisoners. Sergeant Gibson (Mel Stewart) realizes that only the most fortunate of circumstances have kept him from being a criminal and that his position there is contingent on how well he controls the inmates. This is very similar to the black overseer whose privileged position depended on keeping his brethren under control. *On the Rocks* reinforced the idea that blacks engage in criminal activities and represent the majority of convicts. It also showed the successful black male as an Uncle Tom who inhumanly treats his fellow men because of his desire to identify with whites.

Welcome Back, Kotter and *The Cop and the Kid* represent two sociopathic types. This time the characters *were* children. Are these two characters, Freddie Washington (Lawrence Hilton-Jacobs) and Lucas Adams (Tiere Turner), the black men of the future, destined to be pimps and felons that eventually end up *On the Rocks*? It is particularly insidious to portray juveniles as delinquents on television, particularly in a sitcom format. If the show had been successful, it would have many impressionable children emulating these characters, as they imitated "The Fonz," the resident delinquent of the hit show *Happy Days*.

The two shows that depicted positive family interactions and some good role models unfortunately were cancelled because they lacked entertainment value. *Beacon Hill* and *Grady* were almost immediate fiascos in 1975–76, but for their short durations the black family was shown in a positive, humanistic manner. None of the characters were the usual stereotyped fare that is now popular, but rather characters of great depth.

This particularly applied to Richard Ward (as the chef and black father) and Don Blakely (as his son) on *Beacon Hill*. The son wanted to be judged on his merits as a man, not by the color of his skin. Against the backdrop of the Lassiter household and a conservative Boston of the 1920s, a black father and his rebellious son battled to survive and gain dignity, each in his own way, and loving and respecting the other.

Grady, a spin-off of *Sanford and Son*, was less serious than *Beacon Hill*, but it was surprising and refreshing to see an intact black family in which all members respected one another, did not engage in deceitful interactions, had an attractive mother figure (who was also a career woman), and had a father figure who did not corrupt himself (disenfranchise his blackness) in the pursuit of middle-class values. Also, a great deal of respect was given to the family's elder statesman and patriarch, Grandfather Grady.

Unfortunately, the networks seemed to hold little hope for *Grady* or the subplot of *Beacon Hill*, because both shows were aired for less than a season, and no attempt was made to give quality material to either show.

What's Happening!! was not rated on the list because it was a summer pilot and aired for only three weeks. The show concerned the misadventures of three black teenagers. The episodes were complete with unattractive mammies, deceitful interactions, brother-and-sister squabbles, and blacks insulting one another for the sake of humor. More detrimental than any of this was the black family unit with no father, and the only viable black male on the show, the son Roger (Ernest Thomas), was undermined by his younger sister and emasculated by his mother. In two of the three shows, Roger was either threatened or whipped by his mother. The intended message was clear: the black man is ruled by the black woman, and he need not be feared as a competitor to the white man. It is extremely degrading to the black self-concept to be so humiliated on prime-time TV. It is difficult to recall any instance in which a teenager of any color was beaten by his mother; certainly John-Boy (*The Waltons*) never suffered that fate.

The 1976–77 season promised to be better, due to its dramatization of Alex Haley's book *Roots*, the epic story of Haley's family traced back through seven generations to a village on the west coast of Africa. The series was one of the highlights of the season, in part because it did full justice to its source, but mostly because it was the most-watched television program in the history of that medium. At least 130 million viewers tuned in to see some episode of the series.

Additionally, *Roots* was the prototype of the kind of positive images to which this study speaks. The impact of *Roots* was the polar equivalent of D.W. Griffith's 1915 film *The Birth of a Nation* (see below) in the realm of race relations, in that both blacks and whites could see a more complete picture of blacks devoid of black stereotypes and abundant in humanistic, multidimensional characterizations. Unfortunately, many of the white actors were cast in stereotypical roles, which was distasteful to a large portion of the viewing audience. Any type of negative stereotyping is not constructive, but at least a host of other programs give a more balanced view of whites.

However, no matter how dynamic the impact of *Roots* was, the program lasted only a week. The overall positive effects of *Roots* may not mitigate the negative effects of a program that derogates and satirizes the black experience, the black family, and black-white relationships on a weekly basis.

Chapter 14
EVENTS FROM 1976 TO 2017

In this section, racial portrayals will be reviewed by selecting important events this writer considers to be the tipping points that have changed the nature of minority portrayals on television from 1976 to 2017.

The Autobiography of Miss Jane Pittman (1974).

Based on the 1971 novel of that title by Ernest J. Gaines, this CBS TV movie was directed by John Korty, written by Tracy Keenan Wynn, and produced by R. Christiansen and Rick Rosenberg. It won a Directors Guild of America award, as well as nine Emmy Awards, including best actress, best drama, best director, best music composition, best writer, and best costume design. It starred iconic actress Cicely Tyson. It has been called "possibly the best film made for television" and tells the story of a black woman from her childhood in slavery to the beginning of the civil rights movement in the south.

Just an Old Sweet Song (1976)

Melvin Van Peebles wrote this made-for-TV drama for CBS—yes, *that* Melvin Van Peebles (born August 21, 1932), the writer, producer and director of *Sweet Sweetback's Baadasssss Song* (1971). *Just an Old Sweet Song* concerned a black family that moved back to the south, disillusioned by their experiences in the liberal-democratic north. It featured two well-known performers, Cicely Tyson and Robert Hooks, in one of the few realistic representations of blacks.

Van Peebles also wrote and acted in *Sophisticated Gents* (1981) on NBC. This tipping-point production centered on the reunion of nine male members of a black athletic-social club to celebrate the seventieth birthday of the coach who helped them reach success in their lives. NBC did not air the program for two years after it had been produced. The drama featured a host of black actors, such as Robert Hooks, Dick Anthony Williams, Ron O'Neal, Raymond St. Jacques, Thalmus Rasulala, Paul Winfield, Roosevelt Grier, Bernie Casey, and, of course, Van Peebles. They were joined by a group of equally strong and well-known black actresses of the day: Denise Nicholas, Rosalind Cash, Janet MacLachlan, Alfre Woodard, Beah Richards, Ja'net DuBois, and Bibi Besch. The characters were middle-to-upper-class black males who had not forgotten their roots and love for one another. While the script was good, the importance of this series was the assembly of most of the established black actors and actresses of that time.

Minstrel Man (1977)

This two-hour CBS drama by William Graham, S. Esther, and Richard Shapiro told the story of America's black minstrel players during the slavery era when only whites were permitted to perform in minstrel shows. After the Civil War, blacks were permitted to perform in minstrel shows, but they also had to perform in blackface. *Minstrel Man* highlighted the irony and plagiarism of an envious white society that stole this cultural form of black entertainment and simultaneously denigrated and lampooned it—in short, white people trying unsuccessfully to imitate black people while caricaturizing them, according to Eric Lott in his book *Love & Theft* (1995).

Minstrel Man involved two black brothers (Glynn Turman and Stanley Clay) performing shows in blackface. Black entertainers put on makeup to impersonate white performers who used blackface to depict black people. Blacks applying blackface to copy white people is a difficult concept to absorb, but that is what historically happened! The story climaxed when the brothers decided to stop performing as minstrels and present authentic ragtime music instead—a divergence from the expected, not well received by the white audience. In a rebellious, revolutionary gesture, one brother walked among the crowd made up in whiteface, becoming a black man caricaturing white people. He was later found hanging from a tree, still in his white makeup. In an act of self-affirmation, the other brother (during a subsequent minstrel show) wiped the blackface off his face and performed simply as a black man. His fellow performers wiped the black makeup from their ebony faces and joined him.

The drama received good reviews, but more importantly, identifying and accepting the uniqueness of themselves and their culture in the midst of Jim Crow restrictions had never been seen before on network television. In *Love & Theft*, Lott examines this phenomenon:

> For over two centuries, America has celebrated the very black culture it attempts to control and repress, and nowhere is this phenomenon more apparent than in the strange practice of blackface performance. Born of extreme racial and class conflicts, the blackface minstrel shows sometimes served to intensify these conflicts. Based on the appropriation of black dialect, music, and dance, minstrelsy at once applauded and lampooned black culture, ironically contributing to a "blackening of America."

Drawing on recent research of cultural studies and social history, Lott examines the role of the blackface minstrel show in the political struggles of the years leading up to the Civil War. By reading minstrel music, lyrics, jokes, burlesque skits, and illustrations in tandem with working-class racial ideologies and the sex/gender system, Lott argues that blackface minstrels both embodied and disrupted the racial tendencies of its largely white, male, working-class audiences. Underwritten by envy as well as repulsion, Lott exposes minstrelsy as a signifier for multiple branches of the rift between the high and low cultures, and the commodification and attraction mixed with guilt of whites caught in the act of "cultural thievery."

In the recent past, many white entertainers and some black performers have blackened their faces to perform on stage and screen, including but not limited to: Walter Long in *The Birth of a*

Nation (1915), Josephine Baker at various clubs (1925), Al Jolson in *The Jazz Singer* (1927) and *Big Boy* (1930), Stan Laurel and Oliver Hardy in *Pardon Us* (1931), Bing Crosby in *Dream House* (1932), *Mississippi* (1935), *Road to Singapore* (1940), *Holiday Inn* (1942), *Dixie* (1943) and *Here Come the Waves* (1944), Eddie Cantor in *Kid Millions* (1934), Shirley Temple in *The Littlest Rebel* (1935), Martha Raye in *College Holiday* (1936) and *Artists and Models* (1937), Fred Astaire in *Swing Time* (1936) and *Easter Parade* (1948), Mickey Rooney in *Boys Town* (1938), *Babes in Arms* (1939) and *Babes on Broadway* (1941), Marjorie Reynolds in *Holiday Inn* (1942), Ronald Coleman in *A Double Life* (1947), James Whitmore in *Black Like Me* (1964), Keenan Wynn in *Finian's Rainbow* (1968), and, more recently, Robert Downey Jr. in *Tropic Thunder* (2008).

Many white actors wore black makeup to play Othello, Shakespeare's Moor, including Orson Welles (1951), Sir Laurence Olivier (1965), and Anthony Hopkins (1981). Some of them naively thought that, by blackening their skin, they could better immerse themselves in the role of the Othello character. Good luck with that, because being black runs much deeper than simply blackface. Interestingly, an early Othello was played by Ira Aldridge (1825), a black man who obviously did not need black makeup. Subsequent black actors who played this coveted role were Paul Robeson (1930), Moses Gunn (1970), James Earl Jones (1981), Laurence Fishburne (1995), Mekhi Phifer (2001), Chiwetel Ejiofor (2007), and Jimmy Akingbola (2008). Actors Idris Elba (*The Wire*), Yaphet Kotto (*Homicide*), Avery Brooks (*Star Trek: Deep Space Nine*), Denzel Washington (*Training Day* and *Flight*), or a young Sydney Poitier could bring a unique dimension to playing this role with their talent and authentic blackness.

Before we leave this section, an important question must be asked: what was the psychological need for white minstrel plays in the old South and for well-known white performers of the thirties, forties, and fifties to blacken their skin? And why is it that the annual revenue for suntan lotion is $1 billion and, for tanning salons, $5 billion? While people, mainly white, understandably need lotion for sun protection and skin cancer prevention, for others, the flirtation with having, at least temporarily, a darker skin color ($6 billion a year's worth) may have a deeper unconscious meaning, taking them back to the ancient times in the motherland, Africa—the times when their skins were tan, black and brown because the melanin was greater in them and still is in their DNA. Thus, by increasing their exposure to the sun and coming into the light (*Pert Em Heru*, *Coming Forth by Day*) by either sunlight or tanning salons, they increase their melanin cells as they unconsciously connect with their blackness (spiritual selves) from the inside out, as opposed to earlier futile attempts to steal back their blackness from the outside in, by using dark makeup, burnt coke, or the minstrel blackface.

Because of all of these ramifications, *Minstrel Man* qualifies as a tipping point.

Roots: The Saga of an American Family (1977).

The ABC television network chose to present this Black-African television miniseries over eight consecutive nights, because it was unsure about how well it would be received. Based on the best-selling book by Alex Haley, the series was viewed by an estimated 130 million people, representing 85 percent of the television viewing audience at that time. *Roots* became a landmark in the history of television programming. Not only did a mixed audience learn a more accurate history of African-Americans, but it also saw a wide variety of actors and actresses who before *Roots* were invisible to most viewers, including John Amos, LeVar Burton, Louis Gossett Jr., Leslie Uggams, and Georg Stanford Brown, as well as the better-known Ben Vereen.

Roots: The Next Generations (1979)

This miniseries continued the story of Alex Haley's family from the 1880s to the 1960s. About 110 million viewers watched all parts of the saga, which ranged from the advent of Jim Crow through the black power movement and Malcolm X. This fourteen-hour sequel, which cost $18 million to produce, was shown over a seven-night period. It was considered better produced, better directed, and equally if not more compelling than its predecessor, but the original *Roots* will remain the landmark production over its progeny. The cast of *Roots: The Next Generations* included James Earl Jones and Dorian Harewood.

Black Entertainment (BET) (1980)

At the time of the initial study, there were three major networks: ABC, NBC, and CBS. They had a virtual monopoly on what viewers could watch, so one of the first tipping points would be the advent of pay TV. Cable and satellite TV expanded viewer choices to hundreds of channels, providing unlimited options. When there were three major channels, the networks had to pander to the perceived tastes of the viewing audience, which were highly conservative and mainstream. This resulted in a very limited number of minority portrayals that were consistent with the packaged stereotypes discussed earlier. Now, with cable TV, venturesome producers could take risks with niche programming without its sponsors' products taking a financial dive. The product was now the network, which allowed producers to experiment with various types of programming, including those that featured minority performers as *real people*, not stereotypes.

One cable station in particular, Black Entertainment (BET), launched on January 25, 1980, became the major network catering to black audiences. BET, headquartered in Washington, D.C., aired both original and acquired TV series and home-video-released movies, along with hip-hop and rhythm-and-blues music videos. BET is present in 79.82 percent of American households with televisions. In 1991, BET became the first black-controlled company listed on the New York Stock Exchange. In 2001, BET lost its status as a black-owned business when media conglomerate Viacom purchased it for $43 billon, after which it came under extreme criticism for airing programs with negative stereotypes in its sitcoms and hip-hop videos. Of particular concern were its highly sexualized portrayals of black women.

The Cosby Show (1984–1991)

This family-based sitcom was the early eighties' most-watched prime-time television series. The idea of using television to reinforce family life and cultural values is certainly not new, but the use of a black family in this regard is remarkable—and revolutionary—in relation to the way black families were historically depicted on television. *The Cosby Show* epitomizes a program that can achieve high ratings as well as impact minority groups positively. The willingness of a diverse cross-section of America to watch the trials and tribulations of a black middle-class family speaks to the maturity and sophistication of both the population and NBC. We are all well aware of the crisis in the American family regarding absent grandparents, teenage pregnancy, single-parent households, and two-career households. The American family is typically seen as the cause of what is good and bad in society.

Long before *The Cosby Show,* programs like *Mama* (1949-1957), *Father Knows Best* (1954-1960) and *Leave It to Beaver* (1957-1963) were the prime examples of how TV and society viewed the ideal family situation. These shows typified what was best, laudable, and enviable in the family unit. The viewing audience watched and accepted these shows without much consideration for society's cultural and racial diversity. At that time, the impact of television upon the behaviors and attitudes of viewing audiences, including blacks, was not of importance. The idea that television was not only the window to the world, but also a mechanism through which one's identification could be validated, had not yet penetrated the American psyche. Television was more or less viewed as a means of entertainment and a powerful way of selling goods and services.

Black portrayals, however, were a direct result of the primitive level of race relations that existed in the fifties and sixties. The most popular program was *The Amos 'n Andy Show*. While the controversy surrounding the show existed for decades, objective assessment suggested that this show was never intended to exhibit positive black role models or the cultural diversity of black people. The absence of more balanced "black" shows, along with the discovery that people acquire or reinforce their racial attitudes from television, hints at the negative potential of such programming. While black and white families watched the program mainly for amusement, black families did not likely view the characters as ideal role models, nor could they identify with them beyond their racial characteristics. In comparison, in many interracial settings, the viewing audience might think *The Amos 'n Andy Show* was what black people were really like when they were among their kind. It is not uncommon for people to take a well-known TV/movie actor like Whoopi Goldberg or Denzel Washington as a prototype to understand other members of that racial group. For instance, "You should sound like George Jefferson," or "You should look like Halle Berry"—the television character or actor becoming the standard for what a black man or black woman should talk and act like.

In the late sixties, President Johnson's Kerner Commission advised the television industry to integrate blacks into various aspects of television programming, including dramas and sitcoms. In response, 20 percent of major network programming included black portrayals. Unfortunately, a great number of these tended to project negative stereotypes about blacks and black family life, frequently including a dominant, often overweight, black female and an absent, infective black male. These characterizations were not essentially different from the Amos 'n Andy portrayals.

More importantly, the children watching these shows might believe the black depictions accurately represented that racial group. The impressionistic black viewer might find himself or herself in the position of accepting the stereotypes, rejecting them, or forming a more positive association with TV's white role models. This positive identification certainly could benefit all viewers, but it also could carry blacks only so far, since these role models would represent a race different from their own and, implicitly, one superior to their own. A black child's identification with role models from a different race might carry with it an unconscious rejection of that child's racial identity.

While arguments were raised about the importance or commercial value of positive programming involving blacks and other minority groups, no major network was willing to take that chance until *The Cosby Show*. A small but growing body of evidence suggests that black children do identify with black people when they see them in the media, and when black children view positive televised portrayals, they tend to see themselves as more confident and popular in social settings and more effective in academic settings when competing with children from other racial groups. They may also be less willing to accept or agree with negative racial stereotyping.

In addition, a small but growing body of data indicates that white children identify with certain heroic-type blacks on television, thus experience a more positive, if transitory, view of blacks. This experience not only increases the environment in which greater racial understanding and interaction can take place but also relieves white children from having to live up to the societal role of being or feeling superior to other groups. It also frees them from the pangs of guilt, sadness or confusion they may experience when they see other racial groups treated unfairly. In brief, situations of stereotyped portrayals—written, institutionalized, or televised—can adversely affect both the oppressed group and the group viewing themselves as the oppressors.

Bill Cosby was no stranger to television, which potentially influenced the viewing audience. The initial success of *The Cosby Show* hinged more on Cosby's popularity and proven marketability, but its continued success may be attributed to the authenticity he gave to the production. Cosby had black psychiatrist Alvin Poussaint review transcripts to ensure that his programs were realistic and without stereotypical behaviors. The characters were created so the entire viewing audience could identify with the family situation and not feel as if they were watching a black middle-class family. We are also reminded that this American family was black by the subtle inclusions of various aspects of the black experience, such as alluding to blues and jazz music, rapping, and break-dancing when that was popular. *The Cosby Show* exemplifies how television can use its powerful influence to further the progress of racial perceptions while fostering healthy mental attitudes across the entire spectrum of the viewing audience.

Separate but Equal (1991)

Written and directed by George Stevens Jr. and Stan Margulies, this was categorized as a television movie and a miniseries. The film starred iconic black actor Sidney Poitier (Thurgood Marshall), as well as Richard Kiley (Chief Justice Earl Warren), Burt Lancaster (attorney John W. Davis), and Cleavon Little (Judge Robert L. Carter). This was a dramatization of the landmark 1954

Supreme Court case of Linda Brown v. the Board of Education of Topeka, Kansas, which concerned the effort to desegregate public education in the United States, challenging the "separate but equal" rule. The film received the 1991 Academy of Television Arts and Sciences Award (Emmy) for outstanding miniseries. The subject matter certainly qualifies this as a tipping point in television programing and our nation's history.

I'll Fly Away (1991–1993)

Set in the late fifties and early sixties in an unspecified southern state, this television drama series by Joshua Brand and John Falsey featured Regina Taylor as Lilly Harper, a housekeeper for a white district attorney, and Sam Waterston as Forrest Bedford, who took on many capital cases with racial and legal injustice issues embedded in them. Lilly increasingly became involved with gaining her right to vote and other civil rights involving the black people in her town. This highly decorated series won a directing award (Laneuville, 1991) for the "All God's Children" episode and an award for Joshua Brand and John Falsey for best writing in a miniseries. It won three Humanitas Prizes, two Golden Globe Awards, two NAACP Image Awards, and a Peabody Award. In addition to the fine writing, actors Sam Waterston, Mary Alice, and Regina Taylor (whose character rated fifteenth on *TV Guide's* list of the "50 Greatest Characters of All Time") received prime-time Emmy Awards. After the show was cancelled, PBS produced a two-hour special to finish the show's storylines and then aired all thirty-eight episodes. Obviously this show was an artful, highly praised example of what prime-time programming can create, but unfortunately the ratings did not support the continuation of the series. But it is a definite tipping point in the portrayal of African-Americans on prime-time television.

Homicide: Life on the Street (1993–1999)

Based on David Simon's book *Homicide: A Year on the Killing Street*, this 122-episode series depicted the work of the Baltimore Police homicide unit. Written by James Yoshimura and Paul Attanasio, it won a prime-time Emmy Award (1993), Television Association Critics' Awards (1996, 1997, and 1998), and Peabody Awards for best drama (1993, 1995, and 1997). It ranked as number thirty-two on *TV Guide's* "100 Greatest Episodes of All Time" and also made *Entertainment Weekly's* "New TV Classics" list and *Time Magazine's* "Best TV Shows of All Time." This ensemble piece featured three strong African-American actors: Clark Johnson (Detective Meldrick Lewis), Andre Braugher (Detective Frank Pembleton, Emmy for best actor, 1998), and Yaphet Kotto (Lieutenant Giardello). They came to our TV sets every week without fanfare or political message and competently did their jobs, which was message enough. The series also featured soon-to-be well-known actors Ned Beatty, Richard Belzer, Melissa Leo, Kyle Secor, Callie Thorn, Peter Gerety, Toni Lewis, and Jon Seda.

The Bonfire of the Vanities (1990)

In this film adaptation of Tom Wolfe's 1987 novel of the same name, Tom Hanks played Sherman McCoy, a Wall Street bonds trader who underwent a similar change in status. The film is good regarding social status and race relations. Another good read is *Blonde Roots* by Bernardine Evaristo (2009). Her novel explores the hypothesis, "What if the history of the transatlantic trade had been reversed and Africans had enslaved Europeans? How would it have informed the cultural attitudes and insidious racism that lingers and festers today? At the beginning and the end of the day what is most important to understand is that 'all lives matter!' "

Rodney King (1991)

Rodney King (April 2, 1965–June 17, 2012) became well-known (but was not a celebrity yet) after the Los Angeles police stopped his speeding car on the Foothill Freeway (Interstate 210) in the San Fernando Valley at 12:30 a.m. on March 3, 1991.

Mr. King was speeding, on parole, and intoxicated at the time of the incident. California Highway Patrol officers Tim and Melanie Singer pursued King, who would not pull over but exited the freeway, and the chase continued on residential surface streets. Several police and a helicopter joined the pursuit. King's car was cornered and stopped at the intersection of Foothill Boulevard and Osborne Street. The first officers on the scene were Stacey Koon, Laurence Powell, Timothy Wind, Theodore Briseno, and Rolando Solano. Officer Tim Singer ordered King and his two passengers to get out of the vehicle and lie face down on the pavement. The two passengers complied, and because Officer Melanie Singer thought King was reaching for a gun, she drew her weapon. The ranking officer at the scene ordered all officers to holster their weapons.

The officers were then ordered to subdue and handcuff King, who stood and resisted their attempts. He was tased twice; at the time of the second tasing, the George Holliday video began. (Holliday was a local resident who filmed the incident from his balcony.)

Officers Powell and Wind, under Koon's direction, begin hitting King with their batons. Eight officers attempted to subdue King; as a result, he was hit with thirty-three baton blows and six kicks as the officers attempted to subdue him. King's diagnosis at Pacifica Hospital was fractured facial bones, a broken right ankle, and multiple bruises and lacerations. In his negligence lawsuit, King alleged he suffered from skull fractures, permanent brain damage, broken bones and teeth, kidney damage, and emotional-physical trauma.

The four officers—Sergeant Koon, Officer Powell, Officer Briseno, and Officer—were charged with assault with a deadly weapon and use of excessive force. The trial was moved to the upscale Simi Valley, where the jury consisted of Ventura County residents, ten white, one Hispanic, one Asian. The lead prosecutor, Terry White, was African-American. In this case the victim was a black man who had a drinking problem and a criminal record, and his persecutors were police officers, all white, and likely to be given the benefit of the doubt. It was no surprise that, despite the videotape of the incident, basically an all-white jury acquitted the all-white officers. Rodney King was a black man, and he was no O.J. Simpson (see below). He had a criminal record and used alcohol as a solution to his problems. He was not yet a celebrity.

The acquittal of the police officers, however, was seen as the cause of the 1992 riots, in which fifty-three people were killed and over two thousand were injured. Because of the repeated showing of the videotape, the acquittals, and the subsequent riots, Rodney King was catapulted to the status of celebrity along with his refrain, "Can we all get along? … Can we all get along?" It was likely that, because of the riots and Mr. King's newfound status, the police officers were retried by a federal grand jury. At the end of the trial (April 16, 1993), this new jury found Officer Laurence Powell and Sergeant Stacy Koon guilty and sentenced them to twelve months in prison. Officers Timothy Wind and Theodore were acquitted. Mr. King was awarded $3.8 million as a result of his civil suit against the City of Los Angeles.

The O.J. Simpson Trial (1994-95)

If you are a stereotyped black person (a thing), the courtroom and the court of public opinion are not your friends, whether you are a defendant or a victim, as the Rodney King case demonstrated. However, if you are a popular athlete like O.J. Simpson (Orenthal James Simpson), you can literally be found not guilty of killing your ex-wife and her friend because of your wealth and celebrity. That affords you the wealth to get the best lawyers (Robert Shapiro, Johnny Cochran, and F. Lee Bailey, "the dream team") and massive media coverage. The O.J. Simpson trial was covered on major TV stations nationally and internationally because he was a celebrity, not "just another black man." He was a movie star, a Heisman Trophy winner, and a Hall of Fame inductee; he was light skinned and good-looking; and he could literally fly through airports and quickly pick up his Hertz rental car.

Simpson attempted to avoid arrest by having his former Buffalo Bills teammate, Allen G. Cowlings, drive him out of the city in O.J.'s infamous white Bronco. The airways were dominated by the helicopter-televised view of Simpson's slow-speed escape, with a regiment of police cars following but not attempting to commandeer him. This scene was viewed by an estimated 95 million people in the U.S. alone. The pursuit concluded at O.J.'s Brentwood mansion, where he surrendered.

On the first day of court, panels of legal experts flooded the airways with interpretations of what was happening during the trial. Millions of dollars were made and lost because of the Simpson trial. On the day of the verdict, October 3, 1995, the earth stood still. President Clinton was briefed on security measures that would be taken if rioting occurred in the nation, and an estimated 100 million people paused to watch and listen to the verdict. Long-distance calls dropped 58 percent, and trading on the stock exchange decreased by 41 percent. Government officials even postponed meetings. The ensuing decline in work caused an estimated $480 million dollar loss in productivity (Dershowitz, 2004). It was called "the trial of the century." It had all the ingredients of a Hollywood B movie: murder, interracial relationships, celebrity, and money. O.J.'s persona was that of a mega celebrity, to the extent that he was considered a white man. As such, it was a given that he would get a fair trial, but the expectation was that he would be found guilty. When he was acquitted, he became a black man again. He gained some credibility with black folks but lost all of his goodwill with whites. Some thought the verdict had polarized whites and blacks, as if we lived in a country and world where everybody got along. Yet the verdict did not polarize the country; it merely revealed the polarization that had always existed.

O.J. committed the ultimate betrayal; he legitimized the racial myth that the black male's only desire was to sexually pursue and physically abuse white women. He was accepted as a white man, and he woefully and egregiously disappointed the public. He manifested the very behavior whites feared the black man was really about. O.J. had to pay; his former celebrity and honorary white designation could no longer protect him.

In his second (civil) trial on February 6, 1997, the media were not present in the courtroom. Neither his white-boy pass nor his race card was in play anymore, and he was found responsible for the deaths of his ex-wife, Nicole Brown Simpson, and her friend, Ronald Lyle Goldman. In 2007, when O.J. was tried for robbery, assault with a deadly weapon, and kidnapping, he had limited media coverage, no white-boy pass, and no race card. He was convicted again, and he received a nine-to-thirty-year sentence in Lovelock Prison in Las Vegas. However, on July 20, 2017, O.J. was granted parole, and about 240 press credentials were requested for it; he was released from prison on October 1, 2017, after serving almost nine years.

Two critically acclaimed shows, *O.J.: Made in America* and *The People v. O.J. Simpson* (see below), resurrected his celebrity status and mostly likely played a part in the outcome of his parole hearing. There were no white-boy pass or race card, but the media were back. Thus O.J. became the fleeting exception to the rule that, whether you are a perpetrator or a victim, black males and the legal system will likely have an antagonistic relationship. They don't have the celebrity entitlement or the white-boy pass. The stereotypes remain, and the implicit racial bias continues to exist against black males and females in the judicial system.

Trayvon Martin and Jordan Davis (2012)

There is a belief that an unwritten law exists that black males/ black females are being blocked in their efforts to move from zero to hero, as in the Rodney King case. Blacks are typically regarded as zeroes, be they alleged perpetrators or victims of a crime. Trayvon Martin and Jordan Davis are regarded as homicide victims of Florida's Stand Your Ground Law (or metaphorical self-defenses law), but in truth they were not victims, but human beings victimized by the Florida legal system and the individuals who killed them.

What we know about these two 17-year-olds is that they lived in Florida, and each had a confrontation with an older white male (George Zimmerman, 29, and Michael David Dunn, 45, respectively). Neither Trayvon nor Jordan was armed, but Zimmerman and Dunn were. Zimmerman was acquitted of the murder of Trayvon. Dunn received a life sentence without parole plus 90 days for the murder of Jordan, though Dunn's lawyer defended him, and some jurors thought Jordan's killing was "justified" under the Stand Your Ground Law.[35] Dunn's daughter, Rebecca, similarly defended her father on the grounds that "He is going to protect himself if he sees no other way than to bring out his gun, then that's what he's going to do"[36] and called him "a good man. He's not a racist. He's very loving."[37]

As usual, the person victimized was categorized as the aggressor,

---

35   Nicole Flatlow, "Juror: Some on Panel Thought the Killing of Unarmed Teen Jordan Davis was 'Justified'," *ThinkProgress,* Feb. 20, 2014.

36   Cox Media Group, "Daughter Defends Father Found Guilty of Attempted Murder in Loud Music Trial," *WFTV 9 ABC,* Feb. 17, 2014.

37   "Exclusive: Dunn's daughter, 'It should never have happened,' " *First Coast News,* February 17, 2014.

and as such the defendants (the victimizers) were in fear of their lives and therefore justified in using deadly force against unarmed black teenagers—and then had the audacity to declare *themselves* victims. Yes, Zimmerman and Dunn were victims of their minds, which caused them to feel threatened and to consequently attack others in an attempt to purge themselves of their eviscerated self-worth. These mentally unhealthy individuals projected their pathology onto others (blacks in this case) as it has been throughout the history of this country.

Unfortunately, these people have easy access to weapons. Anyone or everyone who enters into their implicit racial bias kill zone can potentially be victimized.[38] We know that stereotypes were the justification for the European enslavement of African people. Let us be clear: no human on the face of the earth has ever been a *slave*; they were or have been *enslaved* by others. While media portrayals and music have never been the sole cause, we will continue to have a racial divide with few or no sanctions against whites killing blacks—in particular whites killing our precious young black men—but something must change.

Yes, the continuance of positive tipping points in media portrayals, television programming, and President Obama's "I Am My Brother's Keeper" initiative are helpful. But what most people will not accept or understand is that we truly are genetically brothers and sisters, and we need to truly protect our brothers and sisters because they are us and we are them. Our children need to be taught not only the dos and don'ts of black-white interactions, but also their positive history and the history

---

38   J.D. Levinson, H. Cai, and D. M. Young, "Guilty by Implicit Racial Bias: The Guilty/Not Guilty Implicit Association Test," *Ohio State Journal of Criminal Law* 8 (2010): 187–208.

of these interracial interactions. Our young men are preoccupied with the notion of respect and being disrespected in reality; you cannot be disrespected, but you can allow yourself to feel disrespected. You can give away your power! They must be taught to respect themselves and, only when their lives are threatened, to protect themselves. Noted black psychologist Wade Nobles advised everyone to respect and protect themselves.

Black-ish (2014)

Reminiscent of *The Cosby Show*, this program concerns an upper-middle-class black family dealing with day-to-day issues concerning families in general and black families in particular. The writers and actors understand the issues and how to make their points in entertaining, humorous ways. The characterizations and scripts are written in such way that the TV audience laughs *with* the characters, not *at* them. Shows like this are a far cry from *The Amos 'n Andy Show* and the Norman Lear productions of *Good Times* and *The Jeffersons* of yesterday, productions replete with stereotypes that did not inform or teach the white audience about the serious issues of the black urban struggle, in addition to being vehicles of entertainment. Premiering September 24, 2014, and running for five seasons so far on ABC, the show features Anthony Anderson, Tracee Ellis Ross (Golden Globe Award for best actress), Laurence Fishburne, Yara Shahidi, Marcus Scribner, Miles Brown, Marsai Martin, Jeff Meacham, Jenifer Lewis, and Peter Mackenzie. The TV series received a Television Critics Association (TCA) award for Outstanding Achievement in Comedy.

The Carmichael Show (2015)

Following the trail blazed by *The Cosby Show* and *Black-ish*, this show was also about a black family. It had well-traveled serious and comedic actors and young newcomers to the field. Yes, the show was funny and highlighted issues of concern for black and white families, such as post-traumatic stress disorder and gender identity. And yes, the scripts and portrayals were such that the audience laughed along *with*, not *at*, the characters. Premiering on August 26, 2015, on NBC, and ending its run on August 9, 2017, after three seasons, the show featured Jerrod Carmichael, David Alan Greer, Amber Stevens West, Loretta Devine, Milton ("Lil Rel") Howery, and Tiffany Haddish.

O.J.: Made in America (2016)

Though it was a twenty-year-old court case, the media still could not get enough of O.J. This five-part documentary on O.J. was produced and directed by Ezra Edelman for ESPN Films. Unlike *The People v. O.J. Simpson* (see below), which focused on the criminal trial, this documentary set out to explore the nexus between race and celebrity. On the surface this was a difficult task, because it was O.J. Some considered him to be merely a black man; others saw him as a black man with a permanent white-boy pass (until the not-guilty criminal verdict).

As we know, O.J. was a money-generating crossover personality. He was a vanilla-type black man who could sell products, charm the public, and not offend black or white people. Historically, very few black men could do that. Bill Cosby could, but, as we discovered, his is another story, another criminal trial, and another felony conviction. Both of these black celebrities can be seen as betraying the public and black and white women in general.

At any rate, *O.J.: Made in America* won the best documentary Oscar at the 89th Academy Awards (2016)—all of this after this man split the public into black and white. The word on the street was that the verdict (in the criminal case) was payback for all unjustly convicted black men. However, we learned that payback is short-lived and has no long-standing value in life or the justice system. Black men continued to be targets and victims. O.J., with his white-boy pass revoked, served prison time for a tangentially related crime, and maybe this was paying back the payback.

The People v. O.J. Simpson: *American Crime Story* (2019)

Twenty years after his trial, here came television and O.J. again! The first season of the FX true crime series debuted on February 2, 2019, with a televised docudrama of the O.J. case based on lawyer and CNN legal contributor Jeffrey Toobin's 1997 book, *The Run of His Life: The People v. O.J. Simpson*. This series received twenty-two Emmy nominations in thirteen categories and won nine, in addition to Golden Globe Awards for outstanding limited series and best actress in a miniseries or a motion picture for television. It was loaded with star-studded actors, including Cuba Gooding Jr. (O.J.), Nathan Lane (F. Lee Bailey), Sarah Paulson (Marcia Clark), John Travolta (David Shapiro), Courtney B. Vance (Johnnie Cochran), Sterling K. Brown (Christopher Darden), Steven Pasquale (Mark Fuhrman), David Schwimmer (Robert Kardashian), Billy Magnussen (Kato Kaelin), and Kenneth Choi (Judge Ito).

Spike Lee

Born Shelton Jackson Lee on March 20, 1957, in Atlanta, Georgia (where he also attended Martin Luther King Jr.'s alma mater, Morehouse College), and raised in Brooklyn, he came to national attention with his first feature film, *She's Gotta Have It*, in 1985. He produces and directs films that speak to the black experience, including *Do the Right Thing* (1989), *Jungle Fever* (1991), *Malcolm X* (1992), *Clockers* (1995), *He Got Game* (1998), *Bamboozled* (2000), *Miracle at St. Anna* (2008), *Da Sweet Blood of Jesus* (2014), and *BlacKkKlansman* (2018), which won the Grand Prix at the Cannes Film Festival and the Academy Award for Best Adapted Screenplay.

Lee's films are factual and stereotype-free and always speak to the truth of black-white relationships, black identity, and the black experience. They are also major productions, employing well-known black and white actors and media personalities, including Denzel Washington, Samuel L. Jackson, Ruby Dee, Halle Berry, Jim Brown, Wesley Snipes, and Delroy Lindo. This writer met Mr. Lee at New York University. When he became aware that I was conducting my doctoral research to prove that the Norman Lear black sitcoms of the day were harming the racial attitudes of black and white children, he quipped, "Norman Lear is not going to like you!"

Tyler Perry

Born Emmitt Perry Jr. on September 13, 1969, in New Orleans, he is the director of black films and television programs. He wrote many stage plays during the 1990s and early 2000s. While best known for performing in drag as the Madea character, he has produced live recordings of his stage plays as well as filmed motion pictures. Many of his plays were adapted as professional film projects.

Perry was able to easily cross over to creating and producing television shows with *House of Payne* (June 21, 2006–August 10, 2012). He signed a multiyear partnership with Oprah Winfrey's TV network OWN (see below) on October 2, 2012, and has created two series for it: *The Haves and the Have Nots* and *Love Thy Neighbor*. His first major film, *Diary of a Mad Black Woman*, grossed $50.6 million domestically on a funding budget of $5.5 million. His other films include *Madea's Family Reunion* (2006), *Daddy's Little Girls* (2007), *Why Did I Get Married?* (2007), *The Family That Preys* (2008), *Madea Goes to Jail* (2009), *I Can Do Bad All by Myself* (2009), and *Why Did I Get Married Too?* (2010). He directed the film version of the 1970s Broadway play *For Colored Girls Who Have Considered Suicide When the Rainbow Is Enough* (2010) and played the lead role as a black detective in *Alex Cross* (2012).

In general, Perry's work has been a milestone of black portrayals in film and television, but we would be remiss if we did not address the cross-dressing issue of his Madea character. There is a history of white actors, namely comedians, cross-dressing: comedian Milton Berle (1950s), Jonathan Winters (1960s), Barry Humphries as Dame Edna Everage (1960s–present), Tony Curtis and Jack Lemmon in *Some Like It Hot* (1959), Tom Hanks in *Bosom Buddies* (1980), Dustin Hoffman in *Tootsie* (1982), and Robin Williams in *Mrs. Doubtfire* (1993). These portrayals were considered humorous and were generally accepted by the public. Black comedians/actors, too, have performed in drag, beginning with Flip Wilson as Geraldine on *The Flip Wilson Show* (1970–1974). Others, such as Eddie Murphy in *The Nutty Professor* (1997) and *The Nutty Professor II: The Klumps* (2001), Tyler Perry's Madea in *Diary of a Mad Black Woman* (2005), and Martin Lawrence in *Big Momma's House* (2006) and *Big Mommas: Like Father, Like Son* (2011), began their cross-dressing portrayals with mixed results. Black audiences may have enjoyed the portrayals, but at the same time lamented over what these portrayals were saying about the black masculine image. Given the history of black stereotypes in film and television, it was understandable why these were accepted but not universally received by black audiences. Tyler Perry, or any black entertainer, was likely not presenting these images to disparage themselves or black people in general. Suffice to say, cross-dressing for black entertainers remains controversial.

Perry may have been transforming himself by cross-dressing not for the sake of humor but to reveal other important aspects of his personality and alter ego that could be best expressed by the feisty Madea. While Spike Lee and Tyler have some conflicts about the cross-dressing issue, Melvin Van Peebles, Lee, and Tyler Perry would agree that what they have accomplished was due in part to trailblazer Oscar Devereaux Micheaux (January 2, 1884–March 25, 1951). The first African-American author, film director, and independent producer of forty-four films, both silent and sound, he founded the Micheaux Film and Book Company of Sioux City in Chicago, which produced his first film, *The Homesteader* (1918). His second film, *Within Our Gates* (1920), was considered his response to *The Birth of a Nation*. His films dealt with the relationship between whites and blacks and refuted how whites portrayed blacks in film.

Oprah Winfrey

Oprah launched her own TV network, OWN (Oprah Winfrey Network), in 2011. Since then she has produced her own shows and contracted with a variety of shows and entertainers, including Tyler Perry (see above), to meet the needs of black and mixed audiences. Given her status as the queen of television talk shows as well as a producer and actor, Oprah is certainly a tipping point herself.

Pearlena Igbokwe

Appointed as executive vice president of drama development for NBC on July 12, 2012, Pearlena previously had a twenty-year career at Showtime, the premium television network. She helped develop the pilot for *Dexter* and oversaw its eight-year run. She supervised the Emmy Award-winning *Nurse Jackie* and *The Big C*, and she produced Tracey Ullman's *State of the Union*, Damon Wayan's *The Underground*, Kirstie Alley's *Fat Actress*, and the television adaptation of *Barbershop*. She was also selected for *Ebony* magazine and Black Enterprises' "Top 50 Showbiz Players."

The Rise of the Black Superhero

Not too long ago, in a place just a dream and a fantasy away, the forces of evil were at it again: plotting to control the world and generally causing gloom and doom. But look up in the sky. It's a bird! It's a plane! It's the Black Panther and Black Lightning! And, yes, they were black. It was not until the end of World War II that blacks were depicted in comics. These early characters were used as background figures—maids, servants, cannibals—and generally presented in caricature. Forecasting what later happened with television and continuing what had occurred in the movies, the comic book industry presumably believed blacks could be best represented as superstitious, lazy, corruptible types who would provide comic relief. Many of the earlier black comic characters had large lips, glistening teeth, bald heads, and/or nappy hair.

A few of the 1940s superheroes acquired black sidekicks, which added to their stature as noble defenders of the downtrodden. This new occurrence, however, did nothing to enhance the image of the black characters. Steamboat, Whitewash, and Ebony, the respective black companions of Captain Marvel, the Young Allies, and the Spirit, each spoke what some linguists call "black English," a dialect complete with its share of "dat heahs," " 'ceptions," "mahs," and "sur'nufs." While these early black portrayals may have had little impact on white readers, they were likely psychologically damaging to young black readers.

Although no strong evidence suggests that blacks identify with blacks they see in the media, children reading these early comics would likely consider these black depictions to be a reflection of what society felt about black people. Additionally, the impressionable reader would either accept the culture's negative concepts of blacks or reject these stereotypical characters and form a positive relationship with white superheroes. The latter could only take the black reader so far, since these heroes represented a race different and superior to the black reader's own.

Complete identification would carry with it a rejection of the child's black identity. Imagine the tragedy of a black man dressed in a Superman costume and rejected by black children as a fake "because everybody knows Superman is white!"

Superman, Batman, and Spiderman are the omnipotent beings of comic fantasy, and, yes, they are white! Clearly, the message coming from the colorful pages of these magazines was that, even in fantasy, one had to be white to be powerful. If one were black, the only way he might gain a sense of importance is to ally himself with an all-powerful white friend. Thus, insidiously, though perhaps unintentionally, the early comics bolstered the self-image of their young white readers while decimating the self-concept of their black readers. In this regard, the early comics were no different from the early black portrayals on the radio, in the movies, or on television.

It was only after the civil unrest of the mid-1960s that President Johnson's National Advisory Commission on Civil Disorders issued a strongly worded message to the mass media: that blacks should be portrayed to highlight their important contributions to American society, emphasizing that they are an integral, viable segment of American society. Before the commission's statement, which was primarily aimed at television, Stan Lee and the publishers of Marvel Comics had the foresight and courage to test the reaction of their readers to a black superhero called T'Challa or the Black Panther (1966). The Black Panther was introduced in Issue 52 of *The Fantastic Four*, one of Marvel's most popular superhero teams. (Currently there is an animated series with the voices of actors Djimon Hounsou, Carl Lumbly, Stephen Stanton,

Kerry Washington, Alfre Woodard, Jill Scott, Kevin Michael Richardson, and Phil Morris.) The "Black Panther" movie was released on February 16, 2018, and has grossed $1.344 billion as of May 22, 2018.

Shortly thereafter, Marvel Comics introduced Black Goliath (1966) and Samuel Thomas Wilson, the Falcon (1969), companion to Captain America. The first superhero to have his own series was Luke Cage (1972), an ex-con who sold his services in the unlikely neighborhood of Harlem, New York.

The time seemed ripe for the emergence of more black superheroes in the graphic novels. Deciding not to limit itself to just one black hero, Marvel created and published William Foster, the Black Goliath (1966), Sam Wilson, the Falcon (1969), Luke Cage (1972), M'Shalla Scott (1972), James Rhodes as War Machine (1979, *Iron Man*, Issue 118) and Blade, the Vampire Slayer (1974). Blade was developed as the Blade Trinity, a series of three financially successful movies (1998, 2002, and 2004) starring Wesley Snipes, and later (June to September 2006) as a television series with rapper Kirk "Sticky Fingaz" Jones in the leading role. The animated version of *Blade* ran for twelve episodes in 2011.

DC Comics, publisher of *Superman* and *Batman* and the comic-book industry's largest publisher, integrated its comics in the public service sections as early as the 1940s, but it wasn't until 1976 that DC's first major black hero was introduced. Machiste, king of an integrated Kingdom of Kiro, teamed with Travis Morgan, the title character of The Warlord series. Together, Morgan and Machiste fought the forces of evil in a world called Skartaris, which mixed prehistoric reptiles and jungle settings with futuristic machines.

In September 1977, DC Comics reissued *Doom Patrol*, with a black superhero called Tempest, named for his ability to conjure up the turbulent forces of nature and transmit them through his body. However, DC's major breakthrough came later that year with Jefferson Pierce, a black high school English teacher and decathlon champion known as Black Lightning, and John Stewart as a black Green Lantern (Volume 2, Issue 87, 1987); Victor Stone as Cyborg (*DC Comics Presents,* Issue 26, 1980); and later with the Teen Titans.

DC Comics still trailed behind Marvel in creating black superheroes, but it introduced several black female heroes: Bumblebee/Karen Beecher Duncan (*Teen Titans,* Issue 45, 1976); Vixen/Mari McCabe (*Action Comics*, Issue 521, 1982); and Martha Washington (1990), created by Frank Miller and Dave Gibbons after they left DC Comics for Dark Horse Comics. Martha Washington, an honorable, full-grown, full-blown, fire-breathing, badass black sister, was essentially an independent freedom-fighter with no superpower save her fighting skills and strength of will. DC had Martha's creators in its hands before letting them slip off to Dark Horse Comics. Vixen and Martha Washington were DC's next two female superheroes, who emerged well after its well-known Wonder Woman (1941).

While the backstory is that Wonder Woman came from a tribe of Greek Amazons in Greek mythology, in fact, the only Amazons that ever existed were African, the Dahomey Amazons, who lived in what is the present-day Republic of Benin from 1645 to 1979, when the last surviving member, Nawi, died. King Houegbadja (1645–1685) was recognized as the creator of this group of women, who later became the bodyguards of his son, King Agadja. They were equipped with muskets and machetes. These women were recruited from the females who would go elephant hunting; they were called the "gbeto." Europeans called them "Amazons," but they called themselves "ahosi" (King's wives) or "mino" (our mothers). Truly courageous and violent, these badass warrior women often fought gunboats, artillery, and the French Foreign Legion. They were frequently defeated but would never give up, and they decapitated their enemies when they won. Historically, these African women-warriors should have been the backstory for Wonder Woman, Vixen, Martha Washington, and all the rest of the black and white women superheroes, for these were real women, not the figments of graphic artists' imaginations. Finally, these women exploded the myths that women (black and white) and black men were not brave and courageous warriors or soldiers in war.

Regarding the portrayal of black superheroes in general, a major conceptual shift occurred: now black males were more articulate and intelligent. William Foster (Black Goliath), for instance, held a PhD in science. These heroes contended with issues ranging from racism and organized crime to futuristic villains.

The comic book industry quickly elevated the new black heroes to a status equivalent to that of their white heroes. The industry introduced human characteristics into all of its heroes (white and black), which made them more reality based, helping young readers to easily identify with them. This raises a question about the importance of children identifying with such fictional heroes and in, of all places, the comics. The answer lies in the development of a child's self-concept. While children learn about themselves and their place in the world primarily from their parents, they also learn from society's prevalent beliefs and values via radio, television, films, printed material, and the Internet. Before the advent of television, one of the most influential forms of media was the comic book. Even now, children continue to read and project themselves into the heroic fantasy worlds comics provide. This identification with heroic ideals gives children a sense of the omnipotence and confidence they will need to be productive in the face of the adversities they will encounter in later life.

Dr. Cedrick Clark, a black psychologist concerned about black portrayals in the media, suggested that the positive portrayal of one's group in the mass media is tantamount to society's sanctioning of the existence of that group, as well as validating it as an important, integral part of the culture (Clark, 1969). Similarly, noted psychologist R. D. Laing (1965) argued that the individual must be reinforced by significant others and the world as being real and alive in order to gain a well-integrated, autonomous sense of self.

In 1975, black psychiatrist Roland Jefferson (1970) cited a case in which a black adolescent male severely injured himself trying to imitate an action scene from the 1971 movie *Shaft*. The youth reported that it was the first time he had seen a black man (Detective John Shaft) who was powerful, and he attempted to duplicate a stunt from the movie that required Shaft's stunt double to swing through a closed window to rescue a hostage. The young man almost killed himself. Dr. Jefferson hypothesized that if this adolescent, and others like him, had resolved his wish to identify with black fantasy heroes at an earlier stage of his life, they would have no need to overidentify with fictionalized black movie heroes. Consequently, Dr. Jefferson bemoaned the dearth of black superheroes in the comics. Positive early identifications, albeit with unrealistic fantasy figures, may give children an opportunity to work through this phase in their development to the point where they can form identifications with real figures and aspire to heroic and realistic goals.

A number of young black graphic artists wanted to increase the diversity of the comic industry by reflecting the complexity and diversity of the real world. They understood that more than African-American representations needed to be presented, because a black superhero was only one of many possible viewpoints to which comic-book readers needed exposure. These young black men—Dwayne McDuffie, Denys Cowan, Michael Davis, and Derek T. Dingle—called themselves the Milestone Group. They knew they could create quality comics, but they needed a professional system of distribution.

To fulfill their distribution goals, the Milestone Group struck a cooperative deal with DC Comics to print and distribute Milestone's comics. DC's status within the industry and its experimentation throughout the 1980s with such cutting-edge concepts as prestige format books, maxi-series, intercompany crossovers, and an AIDS awareness program made it a likely partner for the Milestone Group. Through this arrangement the Milestone Group presented its first titles: *Hardware*, *Icon*, *Blood Syndicate*, and *Static*. Concurrently, SkyBox and DC issued a trading card series, *Milestone: The Dakota Universe*. A year later,

Milestone published its first company crossovers: *Shadow War*, *Shadow Contact*, *Cabinet*, and *Xombi and Kobalt*. Milestone shut down its comics operations in 1997 and is now a licensing company focusing on television properties, including *Static Shock*, an Emmy- and Humanitas Prize-winning animated series.

In 2008, DC Comics announced that Milestone's Dakota Universe would be revived and merged into the DC Universe proper, with Static Shock joining the Teen Titans. The universe was referenced in an animated Batman series as well as several Milestone characters in *Young Justice, Icon* (Issue 1, 1993, featuring Augustus Freeman IV, an alien-like superman who crashed to the earth as a baby), namely Rocket and Virgil Hawkins. In 2010, DC released a limited series, *Milestone Forever*, which described the events that led to the fate of several of Dakota's heroes and Milestone's merger into the DC (Comic) universe.

In 1993, independent publisher Roger Barnes created *Heru, Son of Ausa* (Issue 1), to educate people about the Egyptian-African past through the story of Auset (Isis), Ausa (Osiris), Heru, and Set. The same year, Sandra Mitchell, president of Prophesy Comics & Publishing Company, published *Lionheart*—the original Lionheart (not Kelsey Leigh Kirkland, published by Marvel Comics in 2004), who seemed to be a visitor from the past, steeped in Egyptian spirituality and religion. He was a sure-enough, muscular black man with an amazing shock of white lion's mane for hair. He was called upon to educate black children about their African past and to fight the forces of evil in present-day urban America.

Brotherman (1990) was published by Big City Comics (Guy

Sims and Dawud Anyabwile [born David Sims]). Antonio Valor, an everyday lawyer, decides to make a difference in his city by literally fighting low-level crime with his martial-arts techniques. He attires himself in a superhero costume and calls himself Brotherman, the Dictator of Discipline.

The Spawn was created in 1992 by Todd McFarlane, an independent comic publisher who was formerly Marvel's graphic artist on *Spiderman*. In 1997, McFarlane produced a feature film, *The Spawn*, starring Michael Jai as Spawn, with Martin Sheen and John Leguizamo in the supporting cast; the Spawn was named 36th of the top 100 heroes of all time. An animated TV series, *Todd McFarlane's Spawn,* appeared in 1999, starring Keith David, Michael Beach, Richard Dysart, Dominique Jennings, and Ruben Santiago Hudson. Running from May 16, 1997, to May 28, 1999, the series was fifth on the list of greatest comic cartoons of all time.

African World Press created Captain Africa in Red Anvil Comics' *Najee M'witu* (1987). He wore a green costume powered by the sun, and the continent of Africa was printed on his chest. Captain Africa was the first superhero created by a Nigerian artist to give Nigerian children their own superhero.

In the late sixties and early seventies, there were fewer than ten black superheroes. Now there are well over a hundred, thanks to Marvel, DC, and a host of independent publishers and black publishers. And yes, there is a black Superman, and his name is Icon!

Role Reversals

We also need to walk a mile in someone else's shoes. This process can start by viewing Melvin Van Peebles's *Watermelon Man*, a 1970 film starring Godfrey Cambridge as a white middle-class male who awakens to find he has undergone a metamorphosis into a black male. The film follows his trials of accepting himself and his alienation from his coworkers, neighbors, friends, and family. *Watermelon Man* was a funny and tragic film.

Another good film is *Trading Places* (1983), starring Eddie Murphy, Dan Aykroyd, Jamie Lee Curtis, Ralph Bellamy, and Don Ameche. In this one Winthrop (Aykroyd) is fired from his lucrative job and replaced by Valentine (Murphy), a streetwise black con artist. The company owners have a one-dollar bet about whether it is genetics or the environment that leads to success in business. Valentine succeeds in the company by applying his street smarts to the job, and he quickly changes into an extremely competent businessman. In contrast, Winthrop fails miserably when he has to succeed on his own. He loses his friends, is devastated, and eventually attempts suicide before he is ultimately rescued and restored to his previous status by Valentine. This was the highest-rated R-rated film of 1983.

This writer also recommends psychodrama workshops in which the participants trade racial identities as in the movies "Trading Places" and "Watermelon Man," and are placed in social-racial conflict situations and attempt to bring about resolutions to the conflicts.

Black Actors Cast as the President of the United States

The list begins with seven-year-old Sammy Davis Jr. in *Rufus Jones for President* (1933) and continues with James Earl Jones in *The Man* (1972), Richard Pryor on *The Richard Pryor Show* (1977), Steven Williams in *Sea Quest 2032:* "Better Than Martians" (1993), Tiny Lister Jr. in *The Fifth Element* (1997), Morgan Freeman in *Deep Impact* (1998) and *Olympus Has Fallen* (2013), Dennis Haysbert on *24* (2001), Chris Rock in *Head of State* (2003), Dave Chappelle on *The Dave Chappelle Show* (2004), Louis Gossett Jr. in *Left Behind: World at War* (2005) and *Solar Attack* (2006), Terry Crews in *Idiocracy* (2006), D. B. Woodside on *24* (2007), Danny Glover in *2012* (2009), Blair Underwood on *The Event*, Jamie Foxx in *White House Down* (2013), Samuel L. Jackson in *Big Game* (2014), and Alfre Woodard on *State of Affairs* (2014–15). Obviously the casting of black actors in the role of the most powerful figure on the planet is a paradigm shift for blacks in film and television, which paled in the wake of a black man becoming the first real black president (Barack Obama) in 2008.

With the election of the first black president of the United States, the arc of positive black portrayals on television reached its zenith. The president and/or his family appeared on TV and radio every day of the week. Every time the administration, the House of Representatives, or the Senate was mentioned, thoughts of the president came to mind. When black people were asked, "Who is the president of the United States?" there was a strong emotional reaction, usually positive. Black children who would not know the name of the sitting president now know this former president's name! People of color who are not interested in politics know his name, and they usually smile inwardly and outwardly when they talk about him. It does not get better than this. Even when movie or television portrayals depict the president as white, nobody cares, because people of every color know that Barack Obama was president, and he is a black man, a man of color. The most influential man on planet Earth was a black man; as unbelievable as it is, it is true. A black man in this position had a cleansing, mitigating effect on all of the stereotypes and negative caricatures visited on black people through the history of this world. But, alas, even the president was not immune from racist snipes, including "subhuman mongrel," but this is like water off a duck's back. Nothing, no, nothing, can turn back this mega tipping point!

Tipping Points and Portrayals Past and Present

At this point I'd like to combine tipping points of the past with the tipping points and portrayals of blacks in the present. The creation and influence of stereotypes had the most devastating impact on social and racial relationships known to man. It can be said that stereotyping was the basis/rationale for slavery. It was the reason white people could kill black people with impunity and why black people killed each other. Yes, black people are as impacted by the negative stereotypes of themselves as are white people.

The stereotypes suggest that the person being typed is a thing (thingafication, Kovel, 1970), and that once you have "a thing," you can do anything you want with it. You can own it, you can trash it, or you can destroy it, and because you think of it as a thing, the word *kill* does not enter into the conversation. You can only kill a person, not a thing. You can only feel guilty about harming a person, not a thing.

I offer that, when a human is stereotyped, he or she is being made into a thing (Kovel, 1970), and people are justified in doing whatever they want with that thing. The criminal justice system is not immune to treating people as things. While most people will not admit they have racist attitudes, an implicit bias test indicates that 78 percent of white people and 50 percent of black people harbor implicit racial bias toward black people. Racial profiling is a more sophisticated term for racial stereotyping, treating people as things. Things don't get equal treatment under the law, only people do, and things are not people.

Our society, however, offers things an out, a way only a few can avail themselves. They can become celebrities. As we know, not many people can become celebrities, and even fewer black people can become celebrities as seen by white culture. Early on, white culture viewed rappers as thugs, not celebrities, and the rappers initially liked it that way. They were thugs (things) who made records that insulted women (black women especially), blacks, and white people. Rappers are the cause celeb for adolescent things to play their trashy noise as loud as they want. The performers contaminate, poison, and infect the environment with their auditory diseases under the guise of it being music.

White people, by being white, enjoy an innate celebrity (entitlement) status. They feel entitled and get the benefit of the doubt more times than not in our social and criminal justice systems. As a black person (thing), however, you generally get the raccoon droppings. You have difficulty being properly served in restaurants or hailing a taxi in a large city. You are guilty until proven innocent unless you are a celebrity, a popular athlete, a movie star, a musician, or a singer of what is considered real music (anything but rap or hip-hop).

Chapter 15
SUMMARY AND CONCLUSIONS

This study was conducted to (1) determine the number of prime-time hours allotted to programs employing black performers over a thirteen-year period (1963–1976), (2) categorize each program for possible negative stereotypes, (3) speculate about the psychological and sociological reasons for negative stereotypes, (4) examine the psychological implications of racial stereotypes, and (5) discuss the possible detrimental effects and ideas television has nurtured by depicting blacks as one-dimensional characters.

Three major categories were used to determine whether a specific trend of negative portrayals was occurring over the specified thirteen-year period: (1) *obliteration*, in which the characters were viewed as an amalgamation of blacks and whites—the actor is black, but his attitudes and the storylines and plot situations were foreign to the black experience; (2) *defamation*, in which the program's content calls attention to the imperfections of blacks and condemns them to inferior status; and (3) *disembodiment*, in which the program's content attributes to blacks a subhuman sexuality, depicting them in the extremes of hyposexuality or hypersexuality.

Under the three major categories, fourteen hypotheses were tested and used as scoring criteria for each program selected. A chi-square analysis was used to determine the significant occurrence of each major category and its inclusive hypotheses. The incidence of major category stereotyping, obliteration, defamation, and disembodiment were all found to be significant, as were the following five hypotheses:

H1: Significantly more black actors in white characterizations;

H4: Significant absence of black leading characters on those programs employing black actors;

H6: Significant incidence of black actors in supporting or minor roles;

H10: Significant absence of black male-black female relationships;

H11: Significant occurrence of blacks portrayed as hyposexual.

Of the remaining nine hypotheses found to be insignificant on the basis of the rated programs, an additional five had the "potential to achieve significance" had they been scored on the possibility of stereotypes occurring and not for all eighty-seven programs in the study:

H5: Devious behavior employed by blacks in their interactions with one another;

H8: Blacks in family interactions that are satirical and provoke humor;

H9: Black families presented as matriarchal and/or dominated by the female (mother);

H12: Black females presented as unattractive or as a mammy type;

H14: Strong independent black female characters occurring in programs with no viable black male-black female relationships.

In addition to the hypotheses testing, a season-by-season discussion of the "important" programs was undertaken.

Conclusions were drawn about the capacity of television to shape attitudes and display new ideas. The onus was placed on the television industry to project those images that would (1) increase racial tolerance, (2) give minority groups a sense of existence, and (3) give them a sense of humanity, because, by falling prey to the racist attitudes formulated from the notions that (1) black is evil, (2) blacks are subhuman, and (3) blacks are sexual athletes desiring only to rape white women, television has tended to reinforce these concepts in the minds of their viewing audiences.

To the extent that people need to relate to one another more intimately and not through stereotypical misconceptions, the TV industry has a great responsibility. It must balance its monetary desires with the moral imperative of presenting more relevant, less degrading views of blacks. The images that strike at the heart of the developmental nucleus, the black family unit, desperately need revision.

More work must be done to rate television programs for specific content and to evaluate the viewership's reactions to specific programs. The effects intended and the effects achieved by films and television programs often vary greatly. D. W. Griffith's *The Birth of a Nation* was a notorious example of how a man who, reportedly, had brotherly love for blacks, yet produced a film that not only played on the fears of whites but made those exposed to it less favorable toward blacks (Fearing, 1947). Therefore, no matter what the intent of the networks, they should exercise extreme caution when creating programs about blacks, particularly when employing negative stereotypes for the purposes of entertainment.

Television has developed beyond its original entertainment function into a potent mass communicator of ideas, values, and attitudes, a means by which individuals can organize and structure their environments to allay their fears, affirm their doubts, find alternate solutions to their problems, and vicariously experience ways of behavior that extend beyond the limitations of their personal worlds (Fearing, 1947). The individual may thus take from television what he or she needs or finds useful. In light of this, black people must see themselves portrayed as important people in the dominant culture and must have their subculture treated with sensitivity and respect. The mechanisms by which these needs can be fulfilled haven't been instituted. However, by removing the detrimental stereotypes from existing programs, the networks would be taking important steps in the right direction.

BIBLIOGRAPHY

Adler, B. "You Can't Put That Shaft on TV." *TV Guide*, April 20, 1973.

Allsopp, Ralph N. "Organized Sports: Racism and the Black Youth." Unpublished paper.

Archer, Leonard. *Black Images*. New York: Pageant-Poseidon, LTD, 1973.

Belafonte, H. "Look They Tell Me: Don't Rock the Boat." *New York Times*, April 21, 1968, 24.

Bogart, L. "Negro and White Media Exposure: New Evidence." *Journalism Quarterly* 49, no. 1 (1972): 15–21.

Bogle, Donald. *Toms, Coons, Mulattoes, Mammies & Bucks*. New York: Bantam Books, 1974.

Bragg, Janet Harmon, and Marjorie M. Kriz. *Soaring Above Setbacks: The Autobiography of Janet Harmon Bragg, African American Aviator, as told to Marjorie M. Kriz.* Washington, D.C.: Smithsonian Institution Press, 1996, 1-44

Brown, Les and Pitman. "Tuning TV to Black America." *Variety*, April 17, 1968, 27 and 42.

Brown, Les. *Television: The Business Behind the Box.* New York: Harcourt Brace Jovanovich, Inc., 1971.

Carey, J. W. "Variations in Negro/White Television Preferences." *Journal of Broadcasting* 10 (1966): 199–212.

Clark, C. "Television and Social Controls: Some Observations on the Portrayal of Ethnic Minorities." *Television Quarterly* 8 (1969): 18–22.

Clark, C. "Race, Identification and Television Violence." *In Television and Social Behavior*, Vol. 5. Washington, DC: US Government Printing Office, 1972.

Colle, R. D. "Negro Image in the Mass Media: A Case Study in Social Change." *Journalism_Quarterly* 45 (1968): 55–60.

Collier, Eugenia. "Sanford and Son is White to the Core." *New York Times*, July 2, 1973, 1.

Congressional Black Caucus. "A Position on the Mass Communications Media." Washington, DC, mimeographed, 1972.

Cox Media Group. "Daughter Defends Father Found Guilty of Attempted Murder in Loud Music Trial." *WFTV 9 ABC,* February 17, 2014.

Dally, P. *The Fantasy Game.* New York: Stein and Day, 1975.

Daviney, Edward, R. Star, E. Suchman, and S. Stouffer, eds. *The American Soldier: Adjustment During Army Life,* 2 vols. Princeton, NJ: Princeton University Press, 1949.

Dominick, J. R., and B. S. Greenberg. "Three Seasons of Blacks on Television." *Journal of Advertising Research* 10, no. 2 (1970): 21–27.

Dursiag, Melvin. "He Sees Beyond the Cameras." *TV Guide,* May 13, 1967, 16–18.

Edwards, Harry. *The Revolt of the Black Athlete.* New York: Free Press, The Macmillan Co., 1970.

Elkin, Frederick. "The Value Implications of Popular Films." *Sociology and Social Research* VIII, no. 5 (May-June 1954): 320–322.

"Exclusive: Dunn's Daughter, 'It Should Never Have Happened.' " *First Coast News,* February 17, 2014.

Fearing, Franklin. "Influence of the Movies on Attitudes and Behavior." *Annals of the American Academy of Political and Social Science,* CCLIV (November 1947): 70–79.

Flatlow, Nicole. "Juror: Some on Panel Thought the Killing of Unarmed Teen Jordan Davis was 'Justified'." *ThinkProgress,* February 20, 2014.

Gerson, W. M. "Mass Media Socialization Behavior and Negro-White Differences." *Social Forces* 45 (1966): 4051.

Graves, Sherryl Browne. "Racial Diversity in Children's Television: Its Impact on Racial Attitudes and Stated Program Preferences of Young Children." Unpublished dissertation, Harvard University, 1975.

Greenberg, B. S., and G. J. Hanneman. "Racial Attitudes and the Impact of TV Blacks." *Educational Broadcasting Review* 4, no. 2 (1970): 27–34.

Greenberg, B. S. "Children's Reactions to TV Blacks." *Journalism Quarterly* 49 (1972): 5–14.

Griffin, Adrienne M. "The Relationship of Psychosexual Security, Self-Concept, and Endorsement of Ancient Sexual Beliefs about Black Men to White Supremacist Attitudes." PhD. dissertation, New York University, 1979, 2–191.

Halsell, Grace. *Black and White Sex.* New York: William Morrow & Company, 1972.

Hardesty, V. *Black Wings.* New York: Harper Collins. 2008, 3–119.

Hernton, Calvin C. *Coming Together: Black Power, White Hatred, and Sexual Hang-Ups.* New York: Random House, 1971.

Hinton, James, J. F. Seggar, H. C. Northcott, and B. F. Fontes. "Tokenism and Improving Imagery of Blacks in TV Drama and Comedy: 1973." *Journal of Broadcasting* (Fall 1973): 423–432.

Hobson, Richard. "The Odyssey of a Black Man in White Man's Television." *TV Guide*, March 1, 1969, 18–22.

Holman, L. *Black Knights*. Gretna, LA: Pelican Publishing Company, 2001, 15–50.

Jackson, Derrick Z. "The N-Word and Richard Pryor." *The New York Times*, December 15, 2005.

Jefferson, R. S. "A Critique of Syndicated Television and its Effect on Black People." *Journal of the National Medical Association* 62, no. 2 (1970): 122–128.

Jones, M. C. *Black Son Rising,* 2nd ed. Chicago: African American Images, 2006.

Jordan, Winthrop. *White Over Black*. Chapel Hill, NC: University of North Carolina Press, 1968.

Kardiner, A., and L. Ovesey. *The Mark of Oppression*. New York: World Publishing Company, 1968.

Kaufman, Dave. "Blacks as Regulars in 17 TV Series Next Fall." *Variety*, March 18, 1970, 27.

Kennedy, Randall, *Nigger.* New York: Pantheon Books, 1954.

King, L. *Confessions of a White Racist*. New York: Viking Press, 1971.

Kovel, Joel. *White Racism: A Psychohistory*. New York: Pantheon Books, 1970.

Laing, R. D. *The Divided Self*. Baltimore: Penguin Books, 1965.

Lemon, Richard. "Black Is the Color of TV's Newest Stars." *The Saturday Evening Post*, November 30, 1968, 42–44.

Levinson, J. D., H. Cai, and D. M. Young. "Guilty by Implicit Racial Bias: The Guilty/Not Guilty Implicit Association Test." *Ohio State Journal of Criminal Law* 8 (2010): 187–208.

Lott, Eric. *Love & Theft*. Berkeley, CA: University of California Press, 1993.

Maloney, Martin. "Black Is the Color of Our New TV." *TV Guide*, November 16, 1968, 7–10.

Meggyesy, Dave. *Out of Their League*. Berkeley, CA: Ramparts Press, 1970.

Mehlinger, K. T. "The Image of the Black Man and the Media." *Journal of the National Medical Association* 62, no. 2 (1970): 129–133.

Nicholas, K. B., R. E. McCarter, and R. V. Heckel. "The Effects of Race and Sex on the Imitation of Television Models." *Journal of Social Psychology* 85 (1971): 315–316.

Parrish, Bernie. *They Call It a Game*. New York: The Dial Press, 1971.

Reed, Rex. *Do You Sleep in the Nude?* New York: New American Library, 1968.

Riley, Clayton. "A Black Movie for White Audiences?" *New York Times*, July 25, 1971, 13.

Riley, John. "How I Feel About Being Black." *TV Guide*, February 28, 1970.

Roberts, Churchill. "The Portrayal of Blacks on Network TV." *Journal of Broadcasting* 15 (1971): 45–53.

Robinson, Louie. "TV Discovers the Black Man." *Ebony*, February 1969, 27–33.

Schlinger, M. J., and J. T. Plummer. "Advertising in Black and White." *Journal of Marketing Research* 9 (1972): 149–153.

See, C. "How Can a Square Fit into a Hollywood Circle?" *TV Guide*, August 1969, 24–27.

Shaw, Gary. *Meat on the Hoof*. New York: Dell Publishing Company, Inc., 1972.

Surlin, S. H., and J. R. Dominick. "Television's Function as a Third Parent for Black and White Teenagers." *Journal of Broadcasting* 15 (1970): 55–64.

US Riot Commission Report. *Report of the National Advisory Commission on Civil Disorders.* New York: Bantam Books, 1968.

Vogel, Virgil J. "The Indian in American History Textbooks." *Integrated Education* VI, no. 3 (May-June 1968): 16–32.

Webster, Elizabeth C. "Personality Correlates of Sexual Responsiveness and Patterns of Orgasmic Functioning in Black Women." PhD diss., New York University, 1978, 180–194.

Whitfield, S. E., and Gene Roddenberry. *The Making of Star Trek.* New York: Ballantine Books, 1968.

www.ingramcontent.com/pod-product-compliance
Lightning Source LLC
Chambersburg PA
CBHW070020300526
45794CB00001B/377